THE
RUSSIAN
BUREAU

THE RUSSIAN BUREAU

A Case Study in Wilsonian Diplomacy

LINDA KILLEN

THE UNIVERSITY PRESS OF KENTUCKY

The University Press of Kentucky
Scholarly publisher for the Commonwealth,
serving Bellarmine College, Berea College, Centre
College of Kentucky, Eastern Kentucky University,
The Filson Club, Georgetown College, Kentucky
Historical Society, Kentucky State University,
Morehead State University, Murray State University,
Northern Kentucky University, Transylvania University,
University of Kentucky, University of Louisville,
and Western Kentucky University.

Editorial and Sales Offices: Lexington, Kentucky 40506-0024

Library of Congress Cataloging in Publication Data

∨ Killen, Linda, 1945–
The Russian Bureau.

Bibliography: p.
Includes index.
   1. United States—Foreign relations—Soviet Union.
2. Soviet Union—Foreign relations—United States.
3. United States—Foreign relations—1913–1921
4. Wilson, Woodrow, 1856–1924. 5. United States.
Russian Bureau. 6. Soviet Union—History—Revolution,
1917–1921—Economic aspects. 7. United States—Foreign
economic relations—Soviet Union. 8. Soviet Union—
Foreign economic relations—United States. 9. United
States—Foreign relations administration. I. Title.
E183.8.S65K54 1983   327.73047   83–10403
ISBN 0–8131–1495–0

CONTENTS

PREFACE

Woodrow Wilson's diplomacy, and especially his response
to revolutionary Russia, has been and will continue to be
the focus of an impressive amount of historical research.
Both the man and the era make this almost inevitable.
The man was complex; the era, one of history's turning
points.

   In recent decades, historians have taken a variety of approaches to Wilson, Russia, and the era. Lloyd Gardner, N.
Gordon Levin, Arthur Link, Arno Mayer, and John Thompson have all written or edited books discussing Wilson's response to revolutionary change in a world he would much
more comfortably have seen move forward progressively but
nonviolently. The Bolshevik revolution provides one of the
primary case references and, as a consequence, Wilson's response to the Bolsheviks has been well, if not definitively,
documented.

Another series of studies has explored the economic underpinnings of America's foreign policy (or as some would say, the diplomatic underpinnings of America's economic policy). Joan Hoff Wilson and N. Gordon Levin come to mind, as does Burton Kaufman's book on the Wilson administration's organizational support of foreign trade expansion. More generally, scholars such as Michael Hogan have begun to examine the "informal" efforts at coordination between public policy and private sector implementation, examples of which can be found in Wilson's diplomacy and most particularly in this study of the Russian Bureau.

Students of Woodrow Wilson have explored the mind, motives, and methods of a man who seems to have seen himself in much the manner portrayed by Arthur Walworth over twenty years ago—i.e., "world prophet," willing and able to teach the world how best to behave. Self-righteousness being almost by definition a negative quality in this day and age, Wilson has come in for criticism even among those who applaud his goals.

Courtesy in part of the Vietnam heritage, in part of post-World War II fascination with all things Russian, and in part of the subject's inherent interest, America's participation in the Allied intervention in Russia has received much attention. Much of this material deals with the ongoing debate over why Wilson decided to intervene; less ideologically debatable are those studies or portions of larger studies which discuss the actual course of American military intervention.

There are still areas of Wilson's policy toward Russia which need exploration. In my dissertation, I argued that Wilson, like most Americans at that time, believed that the Bolsheviks were, however irritating while they lasted, only a passing aberration. Consequently, his response to them did not reflect his true Russian policy. Rather, while on one hand trying to deal with the radicals as necessity demanded, on the other he continued to assume that a "revolutionary" —as in the March revolution—Russia was shortly to reemerge. And he formulated much of his Russian policy accordingly. Note, for example, his consistent stand against

Russia's territorial dismemberment. This non-Bolshevik Russian policy needs more scholarly attention if we are to understand the peculiarities of America's reaction to the twentieth century's first major revolution (and, one might argue, most of its later revolutions). One such peculiarity is a Wilsonian tendency to treat various geographic regions in Russia differently. Consciously or unconsciously, most Americans seem to have drawn a line down the Ural mountains, dealing with events in the east and events in the west as virtually unrelated. The reader will find Russian Bureau relief efforts in Siberia very different from Herbert Hoover's relief efforts in the west. And finally, there is still a shortage of documentation on American presence in Russia during 1917-1921, especially nonmilitary and especially in comparison with the nonmilitary presence of other Allied personnel, public and private. Donald Davis and Eugene Trani's work in the YMCA operations in Russia is potentially much more useful in this regard than are the more frequent references to the few Red Cross personnel caught up in the politics of Bolshevik Russia.

The present book is, first and foremost, a study of the War Trade Board of the U.S. Russian Bureau, Incorporated, an agency totally ignored in previous analyses of Wilson and his Russian policy. The bureau's history provides material to help clarify and elaborate existing work on Wilson, on policy toward revolutionary Russia, on public-private cooperation, on economic motivation, and on American activity in "occupied" Russia.

The War Trade Board of the U.S. Russian Bureau, Incorporated, filled a page in one chapter of Wilson's policy toward Russia, 1918-1920. The Russian Bureau was a wartime agency specifically established to provide economic assistance to the Russia of the March, not Bolshevik, revolution. Its creators assumed that, with a little help from her friends, Russia would be able to reestablish economic stability which in turn would lead to political respectability. The help would come in the form of increased trade with the United States; respectability was defined as a non-Bolshevik government ready and able to assume its legitimate international responsibilities.

The story of the Russian Bureau is important in that it adds a new dimension to Wilsonian diplomacy. Untainted by the meanderings and moralities of Wilson's recognition policies, and only proximately associated with military intervention, the bureau was Wilson's primary attempt to let the Russian people help bring about their own political-cum-economic salvation and stability. It is also significant in that it points up so clearly both the flaws in Wilson's world view and the complexities of the world which Wilson tried so hard to mold to his own image.

Above and beyond the obstacles inside Russia working against a successful economic rehabilitation, the Russian Bureau was hampered by an American, or Wilsonian, uncertainty of commitment. One might ask, for example, how much rehabilitation Wilson realistically thought a $5 million government investment could bring to Russia. On the other hand, this $5 million was a pioneering commitment of any government money to what we now speak of as nonmilitary foreign assistance.

One might also ask just exactly what Wilson was trying to do in and to and through Russia. Was he trying to win the war or stop the Bolsheviks? Was he trying to help the Russian people or help American commerce? Was he trying to prevent economic imperialism and exploitation by other economic rivals for the Russian market or simply monopolize that market? These are not all necessarily mutually exclusive, but nor do they automatically function together harmoniously. In his inability to set and follow through on specific and mutually compatible goals for Russia, Wilson may have guaranteed his failure to accomplish any or all of them. The Russian Bureau offers very clear evidence of this vagueness of purpose.

The bureau also illustrates Wilson's ambivalence in relations with other nations of the world. His unwillingness and/or inability to arrive at large-scale joint economic undertakings may have foreordained the bureau's lack of ideological success. Cooperation, on the other hand, may indeed have compromised Wilson's principles beyond his own tolerance and beyond Russian acceptance of the assistance offered.

The Russian Bureau's story provides a case study, therefore, which has implications far beyond its own rather limited theater of operation.

Consequently, I am personally pleased but professionally surprised that no other book, on any aspect of Wilson's policy toward Russia, has dealt with the Russian Bureau. Two of the latest studies, Robert Maddox's *The Unknown War* and Richard Goldhurst's *The Midnight War*, each make one reference to the bureau and/or its personnel. N. Gordon Levin makes none. Even Burton Kaufman's organizational study assigns the bureau only part of a paragraph.

This study of the Russian Bureau is dedicated to Samuel F. Wells, Jr., who may or may not be pleased with the end product, but who is responsible for getting me a doctorate and giving me the discipline to work. I also owe debts of professional gratitude to N. Gordon Levin, Jr. whom I have never met and who wouldn't know me from Adam, but who gave me the first real chance to get my teeth into an idea and decide how I stood on it; to the staffs of the Library of Congress and the National Archives (both the Main Building and the Suitland Annex); and to the Sterling Library at Yale and the Wilson Memorial Library at the University of North Carolina at Chapel Hill.

Doing the research is not the same as actually having a finished manuscript in hand. Professors Noel Eggleston and Frederick H. Bunting both read the manuscript in draft and provided me with insightful comments and critiques. Professor George Herring was invaluable in helping me focus my material. Any errors, omissions, or misjudgments are my own. Doug and Cookie Kliever loaned me a beautiful house on the upper Chesapeake Bay for a summer where I could and did draft the main body of this study; Richard L. Lael gave my ego needed boosts from time to time; Fred and Ethel-Jane Bunting, of Charleston, South Carolina, provided

an excellent work environment and countless contributions
to my peace of mind. Since I am my own typist, I suppose
that I also need to thank some unremembered typing
teacher who covered all those keys with pieces of tape somewhere in high school.

THE
RUSSIAN
BUREAU

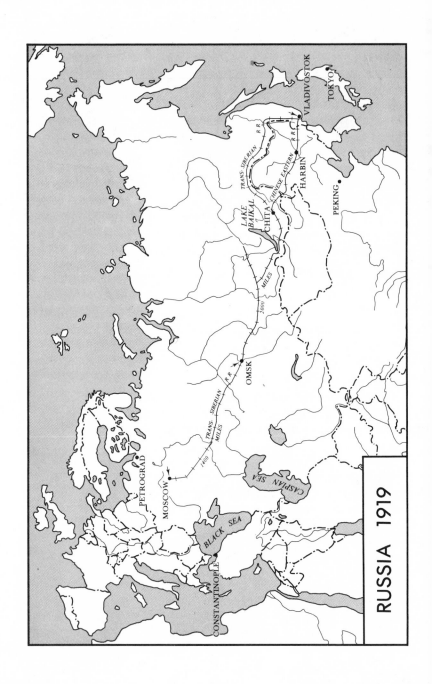

ONE

America and Russia

In the fall of 1918, notices appeared in American newspapers describing a new government agency: The War Trade Board of the U.S. Russian Bureau, Incorporated. The purpose of the agency was described as "helping the Russians to help themselves in stabilizing the economic situation in Russia" through encouragement and facilitation of trade between the two countries. Most of the capital invested in such commerce was expected to come from the private sector. But the bureau would, if necessary, use limited government funds in pursuit of its goals. By encouraging trade, the bureau would "aid in supplying the needs of the people of Russia, in encouraging Russian production and trade," and "in the marketing of Russian products in America and their exchange for American goods." As presented to the American public, the bureau planned "to cooperate with, encourage, and promote such trade with Russia as will assist in the rehabilitation of her economic life." The press releases put less emphasis on the obvious corollary consequence of commercial assistance to Russia: that the successful increase in American-Russian trade would be advantageous to America's economic life as well.[1]

After a long incubation period, the Russian Bureau had come to life in October 1918. For all practical purposes it was dead by July 1919. Its dollars and cents accomplishments were minimal; its purposes unfulfilled; its existence never chronicled. And yet the bureau was the center of a large portion of American policy toward Russia in those trying days of Bolshevism, world war, civil war, Wilsonian idealism, and postwar anxiety. It was classically symbolic of America's ongoing illusion of Russia as a mass of democratic people historically oppressed by tyrants and patiently waiting for the day when they could break down that oppression and join, belatedly, Woodrow Wilson's select "league of honor." Commercial interchange and the operation of the Russian Bureau were expected to provide at least part of the impetus that would bring about such a salvation for Russia.

In spite of its present historical obscurity, the Russian Bureau was not a fly-by-night back-room program about which no one cared. A great many people pinned their hopes for Russia's future on some such undertaking. They saw the government's willingness to appropriate its own funds as a sign of major commitment. The post-World War II reader, familiar with huge governmental expenditures of foreign aid, must remember that such was not the norm in 1918. At that time any government participation in the establishing of trade relations which would make it easier for, in our case, Russia to acquire needed goods qualified as "aid" or as "relief efforts." The appropriation of government money in pursuit of such "relief" represented a radical departure from normal operating procedure. Whether the bureau did or did not live up to its expectations does not alter the importance of such a step viewed in its own historical context.

But the bureau would most probably never have been conceived—and certainly not as a government agency—

were it not for a variety of equally "radical" occurrences taking place in Russia and the world during Woodrow Wilson's second administration. For one thing, in the eighteen months prior to the Russian Bureau's creation, Russia had witnessed dramatic political transformations. In March 1917, in the midst of the Great War, Tsar Nicholas II had been forced to abdicate his throne, freeing Russia from its centuries-old tradition of autocratic rule. President Wilson and many other Americans interpreted this March revolution as a sure sign of mankind's progress toward political maturity. They gave the revolution an importance far greater than its purely Russian consequences would have warranted. One American newspaper announced that, as a result of events in Russia, autocracy had received its death blow and democracy had triumphed. Wilson's close adviser, Colonel Edward House, saw in this March Russian revolution the crumbling of the reactionary old world order.[2]

The purely Russian consequences were, of course, also of great note. Americans now had high hopes for Russia's future. That country showed abundant signs of being fertile ground for a vibrant, progressive nation. Americans found a democratic heritage in the *mir*—the traditional village commune—and other forms of local government, and in expressions of liberal values dating most recently from the revolution of 1905 with its introduction of a limited constitutional monarchy. Those same Americans assumed that Russia's people would, given the chance, clasp liberal democracy to their hearts.[3] Americans also saw in Russia's natural resources and commodity needs an impressive potential for economic growth if a capitalistic environment could be fostered. Under the tsar, they thought, Russians had had little chance to practice entrepreneurship but now, in this new epoch, the time was ripe. Since democracy and capitalism were believed to be the political and economic systems under which America's liberalism had been created and had flourished, it followed to American observers that the emergence of democracy and capitalism in Russia would spark liberal progress of a similar nature.

Most Americans held this image of a democratic Russia when they spoke of revolutionary Russia. The Provisional Government, not the Bolsheviks, spearheaded the "Russian revolution." Events—in the form of a Bolshevik revolution late in 1917 and a civil war shortly thereafter—would, in the eyes of Americans, conspire to delay the implementation of Russia's potentials, but only temporarily. Under the most inauspicious circumstances, "true believers" continued to see obstacles to Russia's progressive development as merely transitory. Very soon the newly released Russian spirit would assert itself and live up to the aspirations President Wilson had expressed in April 1917:

> Does not every American feel that assurance has been added to our hope for the future peace of the world by the wonderful and heartening things that have been happening . . . in Russia?
>
> Russia was known by those who knew it best to have been always in fact democratic at heart, in all the vital habits of her thought, in all the intimate relationships of her people that spoke their natural instinct, their habitual attitude toward life. . . .
>
> Here is a fit partner for a league of honor.

It bears repeating that in contemporary terms this March revolution was *the* Russian revolution. Only with time and the eventual victory of the Bolsheviks did the phrase come to refer to the November Bolshevik takeover.[4]

The ongoing belief of those Americans like Secretary of State Robert Lansing that, in spite of the Bolshevik take-over, "the spirit of democracy continued to dominate the Russian people" meant that two images of Russia competed in policy-makers' minds. The optimistic image showed a Russia compatible with the ideological concepts associated with progressivism and Woodrow Wilson. Many Americans believed that the United States should assume a tutorial role in helping Russia fulfill this potential. Thus, in an article written after the Bolshevik takeover and entitled "Shall We

Abandon Russia?" Senator William Borah answered in the negative, arguing that "there can be no possible conflict of interest between Russia and the United States" and that America should not let the Bolshevik aberration divert it from its duty to assist Russian democratic growth. The pessimistic image confronting policy-makers depicted a Bolshevik power base in Russia which emitted torrents of words and actions totally antithetical to democratic liberalism. By fostering the first, optimistic image of Russia, through such programs as the Russian Bureau, Wilson hoped to speed the demise of the second. Since there seemed no good reason to believe this second, Bolshevik Russia would be of long duration, Wilson felt safe in repeatedly projecting a future Russia compatible with his own goals for mankind.[5]

Literature on Wilson and his Russian policy usually concerns his responses to the ultimate winners of Russia's civil war, i.e., the Bolsheviks. And yet, most Americans did not believe that the Bolsheviks would win. Wilson's Russian policies focused on the Russia of the March revolution, the Russia which Wilson believed was democratic at heart, the post-tsarist Russia that would help the United States guide the world on a progressive course into the liberal future.[6]

By mid-1918 Wilson had arrived at several specific policies toward Russia, two of which clearly reflected this orientation. The United States government refused to recognize the Bolshevik government or any of the anti-Bolshevik regimes that arose to challenge the radicals. None of these power bases, Wilson argued, represented the Russian people. Throughout Wilson's administration the defunct Provisional Government of the March revolution was given full diplomatic recognition. Its ambassador to the United States, Boris Bakhmetev, received all the courtesies due an accredited representative of a sovereign government.[7]

If its recognition policy suggested that the United States was ignoring the political realities in Russia, Wilson's commitment to act as guardian of Russia's rights and interests during that country's "indisposition" suggests a more realistic awareness that the Provisional Government was not in fact a functional power in Russia. In late 1918, for example, Wilson had the remaining American diplomats in Russia make it clear to the local (albeit anti-Bolshevik) authorities that "the interests of Russia have at no time been out of our thoughts and that in any arrangement that may be entered into at any time with the German government, we shall be careful to safeguard the interests of Russia." He had challenged other nations, but especially the Central Powers, to pursue similar unselfish policies toward Russia in his January 8, 1918, Fourteen Points Address: "The treatment accorded Russia by her sister nations in the months to come will be the acid test of their good will, of their comprehension of her needs as distinguished from their own interests, and of their intelligent and unselfish sympathy." Territorial and political integrity were of top priority among Wilson's list of Russian needs, followed closely by economic considerations.[8]

Recognized or not, Bolsheviks and Bolshevism could not be ignored. They threatened the worldwide progressive advances of recent decades. Reacting to the implications of Bolshevism as an ideology, and not necessarily to the Bolsheviks in Russia, Secretary Lansing wrote in October 1918: "There are at work in Europe two implacable enemies of individual Liberty and its guardian, Political Equality and Justice. These enemies are Absolutism and Bolshevism. The former is waning. The latter is increasing. . . ." While Wilson himself never reacted with such vehement antipathy to the Bolsheviks, he must have found it extremely frustrating that the first major Bolshevik victory should have occurred in a country which so recently had taken an auspicious stride in the proper, liberal direction.[9]

Economic assistance could be a weapon used to encourage progressive Russia and discourage Bolshevism. In eastern Europe and western Russia—caught in the devastation of front-line war for over three years—food would provide a carrot by which to entice, or a stick by which to threaten, people away from Bolshevism. In eastern Russia—generally (if inaccurately) referred to as Siberia—the immediate need to combat an ideological threat with food was not so great.

Siberia never felt the full impact of the world war. During most of 1918 that region was even free of Bolshevik control. One of the strongest of Russia's anti-Bolshevik leaders, Admiral Kolchak, exercised political and military control over parts of the region from mid-1918 through most of 1919. And even though Siberia was a battlefield in the Russian civil war and did suffer its own form of social and political disruption, it retained a level of self-sufficiency and local community cohesion. Consequently, American policy-makers thought Siberia provided the most opportune field on which to wage the dual fight against Bolshevism and for the institutionalization of the Provisional Government's Russian revolution.[10]

The first step was a return of order and stability. Americans of the Progressive era believed that, if the communities in eastern Russia could achieve normal agricultural and trade activities and could establish stable local governments, the essentials for a democratic, capitalistic Russia would be able to take root, grow, prosper, and slowly expand toward the eventual emergence of a liberal Russian state. Transportation and communication would be more important than any political structure in beginning this process. The establishment of agricultural and commercial lines of communication and trade would promote a public appreciation for private ownership, individual responsibility, a cash economy, education, and a locally responsible system of government. Americans assumed that the obvious advantage of such benefits would attract other areas to follow suit. This would work toward the development of a progressive and prosperous democratically oriented polity; of course it would also, almost by definition, undercut the appeal of Bolshevism. Lansing, for example, saw Bolshevism as "preeminently an economic and moral phenomenon against which economic and moral remedies alone will prevail." When each individual could feel secure in his own calling, could see profit ensuing from his own initiative, and could be his own master, communism would have no attraction.[11] America's economic role in this process was not to exploit but rather

"to help promote the emergence of a strong and free Russia."
As we shall see, one vehicle through which Woodrow Wilson
hoped to achieve this goal was the Russian Bureau.[12]

Wilson based his world view in part on the moral conviction that the American way had so far proven to be the best
way. In January 1917 he told an audience: "These are
American principles, American policies. We could stand for
no others. And they are also the principles and policies of
forward looking men and women everywhere, of every modern nation, of every enlightened community. They are the
principles of mankind and must prevail." Wilson promoted
America and American principles not because he was
American or because to do so would materially help America. He did so because he believed they were the best principles and because adopting them would be beneficial to the
peoples and countries of the entire world. Russia could provide a testing ground to confirm his beliefs while simultaneously helping a people in need.[13]

For the realists and economic determinists of today, this
picture of altruism is unconvincing. And in fact Wilson was
not totally oblivious to the economic facts of American life.
Rather, he saw the economic, entrepreneurial side of America as one of the major forces behind responsible politics and
social consciousness. Economic activity served no progressive end in and of itself; but it could provide the means to a
higher level of civil maturity and responsibility. When
American businessmen established trading relations with
Russian businessmen they accomplished more than economic growth and profit. They were actively fostering social
and political progress in Russia by developing a citizenry
there capable, for the first time, of expressing and acting
upon its innate progressivism. Wilson's world view both subsumed and transcended the cruder aspects of America's economic reality.[14]

Wilson acknowledged that the Russian people had not
had the opportunity to practice liberal, democratic principles, and he made a commitment to "help Russia help herself." There was little question in the president's mind that

the Russian people would follow American patterns once introduced to them, and his plans included an aggressive exportation of American principles, using commerce as a carrier and a teacher.[15]

In pursuing their plans for Russia, Wilson and his advisers were often handicapped by the unreliability and/or unavailability of information about that country. By early 1918, Russia was coming apart. Under the pressure of constant change, even observers in the field failed to arrive at dependable analyses.[16] In writing that "the changes taking place in Russia are so kaleidoscopic that I feel that information and advice are futile until there is something definite to plan with as well as for," President Wilson expressed a common feeling of frustration. Several months later, in April 1918, the situation had not measurably improved: "things in Russia seem to be in such a fluid state that no definite form arises out of them as yet."[17]

State Department and press reports issuing from Russia reflected the confusion. In March 1918, Assistant Secretary of State Breckinridge Long pointed out that known facts often did not support the abundant rumors in circulation. Wilson's chief foreign policy adviser, Colonel Edward House, confronted any number of "conflicting views" in his contact with people knowledgeable about Russia. And from Europe, America's representative to the Supreme War Council, General Tasker Bliss, lamented: "It is a pity that we cannot get more information as to what is really happening in Russia." Bliss's concern makes it clear that events in Russia affected Americans not only, and not even primarily, on a bilateral Russian-American level. They were also important to Americans because of their impact on the war effort.[18]

In 1917 and 1918 the Great War dominated all else. But much of what happened in Russia had implications for the war and for the postwar world. Russia's fall meant that half of the Allied defense against the Central Powers weakened, crumbled, and finally disappeared as Russia's internal upheavals and war-weariness took their toll. Since the war,

Russia's part in it, and the Allies' response, would ultimately set the stage for the Russian Bureau some background on those interrelationships is in order, however far removed they may sometimes seem from a bureau whose primary function was the promotion of American-Russian trade.

Domestic discontent and continued participation in the war had destroyed the post-tsarist Provisional Government. Trying to fulfill its obligations to the Allies, it strove to keep up a war effort that further devastated the country and alienated massive segments of the population. The United States loaned the Provisional Government millions of dollars; it sent ex-Secretary of State Elihu Root and a group of prominent Americans to assure Russia of continued support in the war effort and in Russia's "revolutionary" new government; it sent a team of experts to help keep Russia's railroads running. The American Red Cross and the Young Men's Christian Association undertook humanitarian programs for Russia. None of these gestures did much to halt Russia's military and economic deterioration. The Bolsheviks took advantage of the disintegration and discontent to convert some Russians to their ideological, class interpretation of the war and, in the process, to raise the general antiwar consciousness of many others.

From the Allies' perspective, the United States entered the war just in time to take up some of the slack resulting from Russia's disintegration. But American participation came at a price. Conflicts of interest and differences of approach would develop between the United States and the Allies over the war in general and the situation in Russia in particular.

War aims quickly emerged as one of the most divisive issues. For Woodrow Wilson, America's entry transformed a war of petty, nationalistic power plays into a crusade for the preservation of good and the destruction of evil. By 1917 Russia was but one of many voices pleading for an Allied reexamination of the purposes behind what had become the bloodiest, most costly, and most disruptive conflict in historical memory. The European Allies did not want to abandon their material and territorial goals; Woodrow Wilson spoke for people who did not want to fight solely to achieve such nationalistic goals. When Russia fell subject to Allied and American military and economic intervention, Wilson would become its guardian against material and territorial exploitation.

Before then, however, the Provisional Government fell. It had been unable to convince the Russian citizenry that the war justified their sacrifices. Lenin and the Bolsheviks seized power and immediately asked for a general armistice and peace negotiations. The Allies refused but Germany accepted this offer. Within a month an armistice between the Bolsheviks and the Central Powers had been arranged, although negotiations for a separate peace dragged on another four months.

After the Bolsheviks issued their invitation to a general armistice, but before a separate peace had been signed, the need to convince Russian and discontented peoples throughout the world that the war was being fought for honorable purposes became even more acute. Acting as Wilson's liaison with the Allies, Colonel House exerted as much pressure as he could to produce a liberalization of their war aims, but he failed.[19]

Wilson's Fourteen Points Address climaxed the war aims issue. It was designed to inspire all participants in the war toward an honorable and just settlement without reparations or retribution. Not coincidentally, Wilson delivered the speech, on January 8, 1918, in the midst of the German-Russian negotiations. But those portions of the address which spoke of the Russian situation may have been more reflective of wishful thinking than of an accurate reading of the realities behind those negotiations:

There is, moreover, a voice calling for these definitions of principle and of purpose which is, it seems to me, more thrilling and more compelling than any of the many moving voices with which the troubled air of the world is filled. It is the voice of the Russian people. They

are prostrate and all but helpless, it would seem, before
the grim power of Germany.... Their power, apparently, is shattered, and yet their soul is not subservient.
They will not yield either in principle or in action.
Their conviction of what is right, of what it is humane
and honorable for them to accept, has been stated with
a frankness, a largeness of view, a generosity of spirit,
and a universal human sympathy which must challenge the admiration of every friend of mankind, and
they have refused to compound their ideals or desert
others that they themselves may be safe. They call to
us to say what it is that we desire, in what, if in anything our purpose and our spirit differ from theirs, and
I believe that the people of the United States would
wish me to respond with utter simplicity and frankness.

Among other things, Wilson wanted to persuade the Russian
people that a victorious Germany would do them irreparable
damage, while an Allied peace would "uphold democratic
and liberal principles."[20]

Wilson's Fourteen Points did not solve the internal crises
in Russia. In March the Bolshevik government approved a
peace treaty which was incredibly harsh in terms of the cost
—material, territorial, and psychological—extracted. It did
stop the world war for Russia, but it did not bring peace. Civil
war followed on the heels of the Bolshevik takeover and
more particularly after the dissolution of the popularly
elected Constituent Assembly and the ratification of a separate peace. The anti-Bolsheviks (commonly but not too dis-
criminatingly referred to as White Russians) began
organizing armies to depose the radicals and perhaps even
reinstate Russia as an active Allied belligerent.[21]

The European Allies wanted desperately to see the White
Russians succeed. Even before the Bolshevik takeover they
had worried about the eastern front. Many believed that
Russia's withdrawal from the world war would spell doom
for the Allied cause. When the spring offensives in 1918

highlighted the advantage gained by Germany from its peace with Russia, the Allies began a concerted push to try somehow—and most likely through military intervention— to reopen the Russian front.[22]

With the passage of time, growing Allied hostility toward the Bolsheviks added another dimension, above and beyond the question of an eastern front, to the Allies' interest in intervention. On June 24 General Bliss reported from Paris that "Everyone here seems to be imbued with a growing and bitter hatred of the Bolshevik Government and, I believe, would welcome anything that would cause its complete destruction.[23]

Americans were much less obsessive about military intervention. Most Washington policy-makers believed that plans to reopen the front would be futile. Under the leadership of Secretary of War Newton Baker, the War Department invariably opposed military action of any kind in Russia or directed against Russia. While the State Department indicated a strong interest in somehow eliminating the Bolsheviks, Wilson himself was not willing to attack them openly. Consequently, his response to the increasing pressure for intervention was shaped not by any desire to reopen the front or stop the Bolsheviks but by the imperatives of cooperating with the Allies and by the realistic possibilities of limiting Germany's exploitation of Russia's remaining war supplies and its natural resources. He, like many others, may also have seen intervention as a good opportunity to begin the economic and political comeback of revolutionary Russia.[24]

In May 1918 Wilson authorized the sending of approximately 5,000 American troops, under British command, to northern Russia. Their assignment was to protect the supply depots at Murmansk and Archangel. Both of those cities, and the region in general, were outside Bolshevik control.[25]

The protection of militarily significant materials also figured in the Siberian intervention, but the Allies had other, more ambitious plans about which American policy-makers were much more skeptical and which made the Siberian supplies a secondary consideration. Wilson ultimately accepted the need for Siberian intervention, but not without long delays and great soul-searching. He felt that military force would accomplish nothing positive, but, according to historian George F. Kennan, he was "sufficiently interested in the Siberian problem and impressed with its urgency, to feel that *some* sort of action was indeed necessary." Perhaps an economic program of some kind would mitigate the negative aspects of military operations.[26]

In mid-July Wilson agreed to participate in the intervention. There is little reason to believe he did so in order to destroy the Bolsheviks militarily. Giving aid and support to the marooned Czechoslovak army provided the immediate, superficial motive for his agreement, but Wilson's decision was basically a concession to the Allies. By early fall 1918 approximately 7,000 troops, under the command of General William S. Graves, arrived in Siberia. This military presence, plus American commitments to supplying the Czechoslovak troops, added impetus to ideas of government-supported economic activity in non-Bolshevik Russia.[27]

While the American military contingent in Siberia operated on orders that limited its purpose to guarding sections of the Trans-Siberian railroad (for supply and evacuation use by the Czechoslovaks) and demanded a "neutral" stance in all contact with Russian internal affairs, the other Allied forces had less circumspect motives. Both major European Allies saw intervention as a way to influence the course of Russia's postwar political, territorial and economic developments to their own advantage. Both wanted a postwar Russia free of Bolshevism. But where France wanted to foster a strong, pro-Allied Russian government that could help block any future German aggression, England saw a strong Russia as a continuing threat to its world possessions and was not, therefore, averse to a breakup and weakening of the tsarist empire. Intervention gave the Asian Ally, Japan, almost limitless possibilities for improving its position in the north Pacific.[28]

Wilson suspected that none of the Allies cared much about helping the Russians help themselves. He disapproved of and protested against the European Allies' nationalistic interests but was even more immediately concerned about the Japanese presence in Russia. In this he reflected common American suspicions of the less than liberal Japanese government and of Japanese economic ambitions with regard to the resources and markets of the Far East.[29]

American interest in perpetuating what many saw as the true revolutionary Russia did not and could not operate in isolation. The world war, Russia's perceived role in that war, and Wilsonian doubts about Allied motivations added international complexities. The emergence of Bolshevism and of civil war inside Russia added ideological and moral complications. Wilson's final acquiescence in military intervention may have made the introduction of an economic program easier on some levels, but it also threatened to alienate many of those very Russians upon whom American believers in revolutionary Russia had pinned their hopes. This complicated collage of world and national events formed the backdrop, and sometimes even sounded the cue lines, for America's first efforts at government-supported economic assistance in Russia.

TWO

Origins of
an Economic Program

In the months immediately following American entry into the world war, the United States government directed most of its energies toward putting men and material into the Western front. Some supplies were funneled into Russia, often paid for from United States government loans to the Provisional Government. The Root Mission went to Russia, in the summer of 1917, to extend assurances of continued American support to the new government and to observe conditions there. Rather naïvely and uncritically, the mission reported positively on Russia's political, economic, and military potentials. Few policy-makers in Washington even vaguely familiar with Russian realities took this analysis very seriously. But the mission itself, regardless of its informational reliability, marked the beginning of Wilson era interest in providing encouragement to Russia's progressive evolution. Any number of avenues presented themselves along which to pursue a closer, mutually beneficial U.S.-Russian relationship. Conceptual distinctions between ideological/economic, moral/material, and military/political relations often blurred, and tangible, concrete plans did not come into focus until October 1918. By then, Russia's distress had been obvious for a long time, as had American interest, for various reasons, in alleviating that distress. Why did Wilson delay so long in authorizing an economic relief program? Unfamiliarity with the very concept of such a government-sponsored undertaking, bureaucratic rivalry over its administration, general uncertainty about conditions in Russia, and a plethora of plans with widely variant scopes and purposes all contributed to the delay.

The November 1917 Bolshevik takeover forced America, but more especially the European Allies, to take an increased interest in Russia. Not only did the Bolshevik commitment to extricate Russia from the war bode ill militarily, but any rapprochement between Germany and Russia might open vast Russian material resources to German exploitation. Those parts of Russia not under Bolshevik control needed to be held safe from such exploitation.

The Provisional Government's ambassador, Boris Bakhmetev, offered perhaps the first *economic* plan to address this and related problems. Even after the Bolshevik takeover, Bakhmetev continued to be recognized by the United States as Russia's only legitimate diplomatic representative, and suggestions from him or his embassy received due consideration in spite of the fact that they represented a government which no longer existed. In December 1917 the Provisional Government's embassy circulated a memorandum suggesting that America and the Allied governments should undertake economic reconstruction and relief measures in Russia. The embassy's expressed concern was war-related: to deprive Germany of political and economic access to Russia. Implicitly, anti-Bolshevik Russian nationalists would welcome such efforts as a wedge both to dislodge Lenin's regime and to rebuild Russia's war-torn economy.

American nationalists might foresee military, political and economic benefits.[1]

This Russian memorandum, raising the possibility of some kind of American economic relief program in Russia, may have been the seed which would ultimately grow into a government agency called the War Trade Board of the U.S. Russian Bureau, Incorporated. But between December 1917 and October 1918, when such an agency finally came to life, many questions had to be answered. What kind of program might serve Russia's needs and with what specific goals? Would it be national or international in character? What role was the federal government prepared to play and what role the private sector? Were the needed "reconstructive" goods and services available? How large a financial commitment would be needed and how much of that would the federal government shoulder? Which branch(es) of government would administer any such program and what would its duration be? The Russian embassy's memorandum opened a Pandora's box of issues needing resolution before its primary goal—relief for Russia—could even begin to be realized.

It should be noted at the outset that the 1918–1919 definition of "aid" or "relief" did not have much in common with the modern, post-World War II usage. At no time was any thought given to outright grants, free of charge if not of strings, for needed food or supplies. Relief would take the form of establishing (or reestablishing) normal free enterprise trade relations between the two countries. Commodities needed in Russia would be paid for by Russians. The measure of how extensive such a "relief" program might be would revolve around intensity of efforts to facilitate or encourage trade. It would not, except in the traditional case of charitable organizations such as the Red Cross, involve grants in aid, or even developmental loans, such as are common in today's foreign assistance programs.[2]

Russia, as a seller and especially as a buyer, already had some trade links to America. Large United States companies such as International Harvester and Singer Sewing Machine had had offices there for years. The American business community had expressed, in recent decades, an interest in opening and expanding Russian markets not dissimilar from its interest in the legendary China market. Some fear of England and Japanese monopolization of the area had already sparked economic concern and rivalry.[3]

American trade with Russia had skyrocketed during the war years, shooting from a yearly average in the low tens of millions of dollars between 1911 and 1914 to an average of about $440 million in 1916 and 1917. However, most of this trade was military in nature and did not contribute either to reconstruction or relief. Shortly after the Bolshevik takeover, America and the Allies extended their economic blockade of the Central Powers to include radical-held territories in Russia. The levels of imports into all areas of Russia dropped precipitously in 1918, partly because of the acute shortage of shipping space for nonpriority commerce.[4]

Initiation of a large scale relief effort would force decisions on such questions as which areas in Russia to target, which political factions to include or exclude, and what kind of administrative agency to use for implementation. As of early 1918 the United States had a number of official and unofficial representatives in Russia, but none seemed suited to administer a relief effort such as the Russian embassy envisioned. The American embassy and consular staffs had more than enough work and some were concentrated in areas not particularly attractive to American commercial or relief efforts. Neither of the semiofficial humanitarian programs operating in Russia—the Red Cross and the Young Men's Christian Association—could be expected to engage in "economic reconstruction." The American businesses with offices in Russia had no official standing and, in any case, were not equipped to undertake the risks or to provide all the bureaucratic support services that a coordinated, large-scale relief effort would entail. The Russian Railway Service Corps, American railroad advisers and technicians under the leadership of Colonel John Stevens, had been helping the Provisional Government improve militarily important rail service in Russia. They found trying to keep the Trans-Siberian Railroad running, even in far eastern, non-Bolshevik Russia, more than enough to occupy their time. In short, the United States had no facilities already available for providing Russia with economic assistance, however defined.

The Russian embassy's suggestion of an economic effort in Russia did coincide, in timing at least, with American proposals for sending political missions to Russia similar perhaps to the earlier Root Mission. These, it was urged, might prevent a separate Russian-German peace by convincing the Bolsheviks and the Russian people of the merits of Wilson's war aims. George Creel, the president's propaganda agent, wrote him on December 27, 1917, that the secretary of state and any number of senators were deluging him "with the suggestion that we send to Russia men of Russian birth for the purpose of explaining America's meaning and purpose" with the hope of keeping Russia in the war. Creel did not think the time appropriate and Wilson, about to deliver his Fourteen Points Address, agreed. The American business community also lobbied for closer ties with Russia. For example, S. R. Bertram, representing the Russian-American Chamber of Commerce, hoped to promote Russian democracy and capitalism through contact with American people and American trade. He wrote Wilson on the subject in December 1917 and remained in touch with the State Department throughout 1918 and into 1919.[5]

These political and economic proposals did not always differentiate between Bolshevik and non-Bolshevik Russia. The civil war had not yet begun; many Americans seemed to see the radicals as a passing phenomenon whose existence only emphasized more clearly the necessity for helping Russia to its political and economic recovery.

During the winter of 1917–1918 Wilson evidently ignored proposals of political or economic efforts to help Russia. Instead, couched in rhetoric of noninterference, the official refrain suggested that only the Russians could bring an end to Russian radicalism and Russian contact with Germany. American representatives in Russia, "diplomatic, economic and others," were told to avoid any interference with that country's internal politics and to be guided in their conduct "by the strictest rules of neutrality." Wilson wanted "to permit the Russian people themselves to work out their own salvation," free from any American interference.[6]

After the Bolsheviks signed a separate peace, and with the European Allies pushing harder and harder for intervention, the Russian embassy had more reason to hope something might come of its suggestions. The separate peace stood to benefit Germany not only by eliminating one enemy but also by opening up huge Russian resources to exploitation. The president and his advisers began giving more and more attention to nonmilitary approaches to this problem. Assistant Secretary of State Breckinridge Long suggested, for example, that economic war be waged against Germany in Russia. Wilson did not think that "practicable" because the United States could not do it unilaterally, and he hesitated working with the Allies in such a venture: "cooperation where ... it is possible cuts in many directions." Wilson was worrying about the risks to him and to Russia of working with Allies whose motives he found suspect. This worry would contribute to his delay in deciding to undertake a relief effort. It also delayed his sanction of military intervention, which the Allies and much of the State Department favored.[7]

In spite of their commitment to winning the war and their dislike of the Bolsheviks, both Secretary Lansing and Assistant Secretary Long opposed the "general outcry" at the State Department in support of military intervention. Long did favor a "civil intervention, with industrial, financial, political and publicity agents." Lansing objected to going even that far, in spite of Creel's earlier report. When, in mid-May, the United States ambassador to China suggested that the situation in Russia was favorable for "effective joint action of Allies and American initiative" and that a moderately financed commission might be able to "reconstruct at least Siberia as an Allied factor," the secretary argued that the time was not yet right.[8]

Lansing's negative response to such ideas was based not on their relief proposals but rather on their military objectives. By May, and like both the president and the secretary of war, Lansing saw little chance of Russia reentering the war. He did see political and economic benefits accruing from a stabilized (i.e., anti-Bolshevik) Russia. Basil Miles and J. Butler Wright, both department experts on Russia, worked on plans for a nonmilitary way to encourage Russia in that direction. Miles and Wright outlined proposals for economic assistance—as opposed to war—either singly or as a supplement to military intervention. Miles wanted to send several hundred Russian-Americans to Russia to counteract German propaganda. More railway advisers should be sent to supplement the Russian Railway Service Corps. Fifty business, financial, mining, and agricultural expert fact finders could go to Russia, analyze its needs, and "help untangle the industrial and financial chaos produced by the Bolsheviks." Miles wanted licenses granted to encourage trade between the United States and the large and economically important Russian cooperative societies, particularly for goods which had military value and which might otherwise end up in German hands. In addition, the United States could provide relief supplies and continue Red Cross and YMCA activities. Miles also suggested that "the assistance on the economic side might well be centered in a small Allied Mission of very distinguished liberals which would command public sympathy and confidence."[9]

Wright, modifying Miles's proposals, saw an expanded Russian Railway Service Corps as the nucleus for "Allied economic assistance to Russia and reorganization of her resources." Military troops would be used only to protect the railroad and the economic mission. His proposals, for which he gave Miles much credit, also emphasized the educational goals of such a program, agriculturally and technically.[10]

Both Miles and Wright used the terms "American" and "Allied" interchangeably, making it difficult to know whether they were contemplating a purely American undertaking or a joint program. Neither proposal went into detail on who would provide the necessary financing. There is also no clear indication of who and what they were including in their definition of Russia, but it seems safe to assume that the missions proposed would not be working closely with the Bolsheviks.

President Wilson displayed an unwillingness to deal with the Bolsheviks. In June 1918 the White House authorized the use of approximately $6 million (the so-called "Francis Fund") by America's ambassador to Russia, David Francis, to purchase war materiel in Russia before it could be expropriated by the enemy. Wilson's only fear was that the United States would spend what he considered "real money" in this program and then have the supplies fall into German or "irresponsible" Bolshevik hands anyway. By the time a more coordinated economic policy had been defined in late 1918, most of the Francis Fund money had been expended. It never constituted an integral part of any projected economic assistance effort.[11] But the student of such efforts might take note of the insight Wilson's comment provides. Purchase of military supplies represented an unquestionably legitimate expenditure of government funds. If the president thought $6 million for this purpose constituted "real money," how much money would he be willing to commit to a much more experimental and traditionally nongovernmental economic relief undertaking?

Most of the early 1918 proposals had focused on missions going to Russia. But by late May, Colonel House wanted to establish an interdepartmental board in Washington to disseminate information and centralize policy pertaining to Russia. House did not think the State Department capable of the job: "The subject is so vast, the ramifications so far-reaching, that only through some [other] organization can the problems arising be properly brought to [the president's] attention."[12] This sounds like a criticism of the State Department and Lansing. In fact, House had a good deal of respect for Lansing but knew that Wilson did not. If the president was to give Russian problems his full attention, he had to be briefed by someone to whom he would listen. Lansing was not the man. Secretary of Commerce William Redfield, as the government official most in contact with those American businesses that would be providing "relief," seemed a likely candidate, but House did not like Redfield or his department. The colonel was too busy to take on the job himself. He may well have looked to the war bureaucracy most logically interested in things relating to Russia: the War Trade Board.

Created in 1917, along with a network of war bureaucracies to integrate and coordinate the private sector's participation in the war effort, the War Trade Board's specific responsibility was the regulation, through licensing, of international trade and commerce. At its peak, the board controlled all goods entering or leaving the United States and actively encouraged American economic expansion overseas. Wilson appointed Vance McCormick, former Pennsylvania newspaper editor and active Democratic party member, to head this agency. McCormick would later go to Paris with Wilson as a special adviser to the peace delegation and seems to have had Wilson's full confidence.[13] McCormick's aide-de-camp at the War Trade Board was a young man named John Foster Dulles.

On June 5, 1918, a committee appointed by the War Trade Board to explore ways of facilitating trade with Russia made its report. It is not immediately evident where the idea for a War Trade Board study originated, but it is not inconceivable that Colonel House played a role. The report deserves detailed summarization, both in its own right and in light of the War Trade Board's role in creating an economic relief program to assist Russia.[14]

According to the report's authors, Germany had made inroads in Russia by supporting secessionist movements in exchange for economic and commercial concessions inside the territories controlled by such movements. Similar tactics would probably continue to be successful "unless prompt steps are taken to straighten out the economic and financial situation, because the conservative minority [in Russia], however little they may desire German exploitation, will prefer it to the financial and physical chaos reigning at present." The Germans also dealt directly with the Bolsheviks in their search for access to Russia's resources. The board did not want to see Russia, now out of the war, become a supplier of German needs. Therefore, the United States should seek to create conditions in Russia "so that the blockade of the Central Powers which the War Trade Board is enforcing by commercial agreements with western European neutrals will in Russia also be maintained." The obvious way to deprive Germany was to substitute the United States as purchaser and supplier of Russia's goods and needs. In the War Trade Board planners' minds, this objective ranked high enough to justify contingency plans for dealing with the Bolsheviks if necessary. As we shall see, the War Trade Board and the State Department disagreed about how to handle the Bolsheviks; the State Department advocated a total absence of contact. While the War Trade Board did not spell it out, Wilson's policy in support of Russia's territorial integrity precluded America's emulation of German tactics in the generally non-Bolshevik separatist areas of Russia.[15]

The War Trade Board committee stressed that "there should be no thought of money making but commodity for commodity of equal value should be the rule." Losses should be accepted "unhesitatingly" if they serve "the interests of humanity or secure the confidence of the Russian people." The report does not make it clear whether the United States government or the private sector was expected to absorb such losses. The committee believed that any American plans must take account of prevalent Russian attitudes toward the war and the Allies. The Russians felt that they had already made extraordinary sacrifices in the Allies' cause and were now receiving unjust criticism. They had been forced to leave the war because "their destitute condition . . . made any other course impossible." The Soviet government also thought some of the movements trying to overthrow it received aid and encouragement from the British and French. The whole country deplored any possibility "of Japanese invasion" and felt suspicious of offers of help coming from England, France, or Japan. On the other hand, because of President Wilson's "expressions of sympathy and well known democratic ideals," Russians (and Bolsheviks) would probably welcome offers of assistance by the United States.[16]

It bears repeating that the War Trade Board seemed willing to deal with the Bolsheviks if that would undercut German exploitation. The State Department favored ostracism of the radicals as a means of forcing them to break with Germany. This may simply reflect variation in method; it may also be that the State Department had seen a way to have economic means serve both military and political goals, whereas the War Trade Board dealt more apolitically with achieving economic and military goals.

After highlighting Russia's economic significance, the War Trade Board committee urged economic action for the following reasons: (1) to fulfill humanitarian needs; (2) to obtain, in exchange for needed supplies or by purchase, raw materials important to the war effort; (3) to keep those same supplies from falling into German hands; (4) to prevent "migration of man power" from Russia to the Central Powers; (5) to "prevent the enemy from securing permanent hold upon Russian economic resources and commercial opportunities"; and (6) to "prevent Russian acceptance of German political leadership." Although the War Trade Board had regulatory responsibilities limited to the duration of the war, its staff did project American interests past that time frame and recognized the importance of long-range planning for Russia's economic future.[17]

To implement its recommendations the committee suggested the appointment of a Washington-based commissioner (similar to House's idea)—"all matters pertaining to Russia to center in him in the future"—with an extensive support staff. In addition, a group of experts should go to

Russia and create, westward from Vladivostok along the Trans-Siberian, an organization to promote the distribution of those commodities "which the Russian people most urgently require" in exchange for whatever domestic products they might have. These experts most probably would deal with Russia's cooperative societies, which might prove to be very helpful in this enterprise.[18]

The task ahead would not be easy. The committee's report pinpointed certain Russian problem areas. An "almost complete breakdown in transportation facilities," which made distribution of goods unequal and in some cases impossible, was only exacerbated by a deterioration of the currency to such an extent that most Russians would "refuse to exchange their commodities" for rubles and consequently were relying on the barter system. There was a general shortage of finished articles, especially clothing, caused by both the distribution problems and the cessation of manufacture (which in turn was largely a result of the transportation problems). Certain areas suffered from a shortage of seed grain.[19]

After reviewing the committee's report, officials of the War Trade Board endorsed the recommendations and forwarded the report to the State Department for consideration. The War Trade Board had done a very good job of picking out the major obstacles to successfully increasing trade with Russia.

The same week that the War Trade Board sent its report to the State Department, the Commerce Department learned that economic plans for Russia were in the wind, probably through unofficial contacts with Basil Miles. On June 8, Secretary William Redfield sent Wilson an unsolicited letter in which he made three points: (1) he had information which led him to believe that the United States had both "the opportunity and . . . the obligation to make [its] influence felt through commercial lines in helpfulness to the Russian people"; (2) his department had access to much information on Russia not available to other branches of the government; and (3) his department was ready and willing to act, "and we believe we understand what the situation requires." Redfield wanted the Commerce Department involved in any commercial program for Russia undertaken by the United States government. This is just what Colonel House had not wanted.[20]

It was also not what the State Department wanted. Rivalry and differences of approach characterized the relationship between the Commerce and State departments. They were currently in a battle over whether the consular offices around the world should report to the Commerce Department as well as the State Department, or just to the State Department. Lansing and his staff would try to cut Redfield out of any Russian adventures if they could do so.[21]

Wilson must have known all of this, and yet he accepted Redfield's offer to cooperate. In fact, during much of June the president referred to Redfield as the person "with whom and through him [sic] I am trying to make arrangements for Russia." Wilson seems to have been playing Commerce and State off against each other, getting advice from both but rarely bringing the two together. This may have been an attempt to garner the best ideas from both. Or, given Wilson's desire to hand much of any relief effort commercial activity over to the private sector, he may have seen Commerce as the logical liaison. Or it may simply have been symptomatic of a general lack of coordination on things Russia. Whatever the case, during June 1918 most of the thinking Wilson did on Russian economic ideas was done in a Commerce Department context.[22]

A meeting between Wilson and Redfield "for the purpose of seeing if we can't between us organize an original kind of relief expedition for Russia" took place on June 25. Wilson had envisioned an organization of private interests engaging in barter commerce—"the only sort that [he felt was] now feasible"—with government providing controls and advice. But Redfield pointed out that if commercial interests operated entirely on their private account the Germans could charge that "we entered Russia for business profit and that whatever else was done has as its ultimate basis profiteering." In truth, Redfield doubted whether he could find participants *not* primarily interested in profit. He suggested setting up a public commercial corporation with a capital investment of about $100 million. With that much money, the government could itself engage in the trade, thus guaranteeing reasonable pricing.[23]

Wilson rejected this suggestion. Use of government funds seemed to him "for the present at any rate, out of the question." Any relief program would need financing by the private sector. Profiteering could be avoided by skillful application of government "influence and guidance." On the other hand, Wilson did not want private interests initiating commercial programs in Russia without official authorization. Although Redfield might well have harbored doubts about the business community's receptivity, by June 28 he had arrived at a working proposal which might have won Wilson's approval. But before that happened the Commerce Department ran afoul of the State Department.[24]

While Redfield discussed plans with Wilson, the State Department continued to plot its own course, apparently oblivious to the president's Commerce Department focus. On June 14 Basil Miles gave the War Trade Board's report a favorable critique but noted that Assistant Secretary of State Frank Polk "was rather inclined to take exception to the W.T.B. butting in on this." Not surprisingly, therefore, the State Department would also resent Redfield's efforts to involve the Commerce Department.[25]

Colonel House now worked actively with the State Department to develop an alternative, non-Commerce-centered, Russian program. Gordon Auchincloss, on the State Department's staff and also House's son-in-law, served as informal liaison between the colonel and the department. With House's approval, Auchincloss drafted the letter Lansing sent to Wilson on June 13 calling for the creation of a commission which would initiate an "eagerly await[ed]" plan to meet the present chaotic conditions in Russia and "give some tangible evidence to the world that the United States proposed to stand by Russia and to assist the Russian people" in these trying times.[26]

On June 19 Auchincloss heard, second hand, that Wilson was working on a plan involving "the barter and exchange of commodities in Russia." He wrongly assumed that Wilson had accepted the June 13 House-Auchincloss-Lansing suggestions and hoped the president would "hurry up and act." Two days later Auchincloss lamented that "the matter of the most interest at the present time is the Russian situation, and no one seems to know what the President is going to do."[27]

In fact, the president was giving the Russian situation much of his attention, but he was not doing it through the State Department. That some kind of plan had emerged from the meetings with Redfield was apparent when, on June 28, the secretary of commerce suggested to the president that, with due care taken to preserve the confidentiality of "the policy," the Shipping, War Trade, and War Industries boards plus the Treasury Department be informed so that they would approve the necessary licenses for shipments to Siberia. The State Department was glaringly missing from the list of those agencies with a need to know. When the outline of this plan appeared in the *Washington Post*, Lansing took the opportunity dramatically to undercut Redfield's influence on Russian policy. He did so with apparent disregard for how such a contretemps might retard *any* plans for Russia.[28]

On June 29 the *Washington Post* reported nonspecific plans for a proposed economic mission to Russia. The report might have been interpreted to imply the government's willingness to let businessmen exploit Russia's plight. Lansing immediately called Wilson for clarification and, when Wilson apparently pleaded ignorance, conducted an investigation to find out more about the story. The State Department had not been the paper's source. Nor had the story referred to the Lansing-Auchincloss-House proposals. Implying that any other plans were news to him, Lansing informed the presumably uninformed president that he, Lansing, had just heard, from two unnamed persons, of the Commerce Department's plan and of a desire on that department's part not to let the State Department "meddle." Fuming at what he saw as a usurpation of State Department interests, Lansing magnanimously assured Wilson that he did not believe the leak to be Redfield's fault but rather that of some power-hungry subordinates. Lansing was "sure" Redfield would want to cooperate and not "monopolize" the work of any mission to Russia. To this end, and apparently thinking in terms of a private sector commission rather than a government agency, Lansing suggested the establishment of a "subsidiary [governmental] council to analyze and study the work of the commission and in a measure regulate it." Here was an obvious role for the State Department and a way to ameliorate the "unfortunate" impression which a primarily private sector commission would make.

Since Wilson himself had been insistent upon leaving much of the responsibility in private hands, Lansing's browbeating of the Commerce Department was a little unfair, but it did have the desired effect: no further references to this particular Redfield plan. On the other hand, no alternative plans won immediate presidential support. Wilson had been thinking along the lines of a primarily private sector relief effort. When that idea backfired, he seems to have had no ready substitute, especially given his reluctance to use government money. As a result, economic planning for Russia drifted.[29]

In July 1918, seven months after the Bolshevik call for an armistice and the consequent disappearance of an eastern front, Wilson finally agreed to military intervention in Russia. Since the American troop contingent would reach Vladivostok by August, this meant that any economic mission would now follow in the wake of the military. In belated reply to several of House's communiqués, Wilson explained that "I have not written recently because I have been sweating blood over the question what is right and feasible *(possible)* to do in Russia. It goes to pieces like quicksilver under my touch." He hoped, however, to be able to report progress "presently, along the double line of economic assistance and aid to the Czecho-Slovacs."[30] Gordon Auchincloss imposed his own interpretation on events when he reported, after a meeting with Wilson, Lansing, and the top military leaders, that a small contingent of American and Japanese troops was to be sent "to protect an economic mission to Russia." Certainly, when the world learned of America's acquiescence in military intervention on July 17, the military aspects received primary billing—not the economic.[31]

The official announcement, in the form of an *aide-mémoire* to the Allies, of America's agreement to participate on a limited scale in military intervention in Russia clearly stated that any economic program was in no way to upstage or embarrass the military operations. In fact, reference to plans for economic operations came only in the concluding paragraph:

> It is the hope and purpose of the Government of the United States to take advantage of the earliest opportunity to send to Siberia a commission of merchants, agricultural experts, labor advisers, Red Cross representatives, and agents of the Young Men's Christian Association accustomed to organizing the best methods of spreading useful information and rendering educational help of a modest sort, in order in some systematic manner to relieve the immediate economic necessities of the people there in every way for which opportunity may open.

No firm arrangements had yet been made—which is understandable given the discrepancies between this rather missionary-sounding proposal and both the War Trade Board's and Redfield's more commercially oriented plans.[32]

During the next six weeks, although a few of Wilson's advisers welcomed his unwillingness to act precipitously, others regretted the continued delay. Redfield, apparently unaware of his fall from grace, was now considering a trading post plan which would overcome the shortage of credit and fiscal facilities by exchanging goods on a barter system.

He regularly replied to queries about Russia that everybody was waiting for the president.[33]

When Colonel House finally got a chance to discuss Russia with the president, Wilson saw no need for haste "because he believed the military forces should go in before the economic." House disagreed, to his diary if not necessarily to the president: "My opinion is that he has done the whole thing badly. I would have featured the economic part of it and sent in that section before the military, or at least have co-operated with it."[34]

The Allies were no more pleased with Wilson's delay than was House, and they pressed for information on American plans. Lansing hedged, suggesting that too detailed coordination would hinder prompt action when needed. In mid-August, the State Department wrote, and Wilson approved for transmittal, another negative reply to British overtures:

> The United States Government appreciates the offer to cooperate on the part of the British Government. It is apparent, however, that the British Government believes the United States Government has in mind a purely economic mission rather than a mission which would have for its main object the study of the situation and would endeavor to ascertain in what way the Russian could be assisted to help himself. In other words, the Red Cross and educational side of the mission would be very much more to the fore than the economic side.

If that really was the British perception, here was evidence of the "unfavorable" impression Lansing had feared would result from publicity about Redfield's earlier proposal. On the other hand, such a perception was not far removed from the final product, i.e., the Russian Bureau. In any case, since neither the personnel nor the details of any mission had yet been worked out, the United States government understandably would not discuss the operational questions broached by the British. Auchincloss's suggestion that the Allies be advised that details would not be discussed until a chief of mission had been appointed was implemented in late August. This evasiveness did not help allay Allied suspicions that America wanted to keep its plans and programs separate and apart from the general Allied effort.[35]

Those suspicions were well grounded. Wilson complained that the Allies refused to make the distinction between politics and economics he felt was so vital to preserving the Russian integrity. In August he had Lansing tell them, rather bluntly, that the United States would not cooperate in political action. He added: "The more plain and emphatic this is made the less danger will there be of subsequent misunderstandings and irritations." Auchincloss softened this rather sharp statement with repeated assurances that the United States would support economic cooperation in Siberia. But, since the United States did not yet *have* any concrete economic plans, as Auchincloss was reluctantly forced to admit, such cooperation would have to wait a while. Shortly thereafter, Secretary Lansing warded off a proposed inter-Allied economic council with the blithe assurance that naturally everyone would cooperate when the time came and, consequently, that no formal arrangements were needed now.[36]

One cannot help wondering just how much cooperation could ever be possible given Wilson's perception of Allied motives and his commitment to guarding Russia against outside exploitation. His conviction that America was uniquely suited to providing sincere and altruistic assistance did get reinforcement from other sources, making it difficult to credit this self-righteousness to Wilson alone.

In August 1918 P. Batolin, a White Russian financier, made the rounds in Washington fostering Russian-American economic and financial friendship. Nothing of commercial note emerged at the time, but Batolin did impress on Americans the scope of present and future economic opportunity in Russia. He also bolstered the American ego by urging that assistance come from the United States and not from the Allies, whom, he reported, the Russian population distrusted.[37] International Harvester's Cyrus McCormick repeated similar sentiments in a September 13 letter to Wilson. A member of the 1917 Root Mission and chairman of a company with long time and extensive dealings in Russia, McCormick considered himself something of a Russian expert. He insisted that whatever cooperation might come from the Allies, leadership of any economic program should be American: "The Russians trust America for having no ulterior object in view. They do not trust England, France, or Japan to the same extent."[38]

Trusted or not, the British pursued their own economic plans for Russia. On September 3, 1918, the British embassy informed the State Department of the establishment of a business organization which would act as the government's agent in supplying goods to Siberia. Although the motivations behind such an organization seemed (on paper) at least as pure in heart as those of the United States, America did not then—nor did it at any time in the future—evince much interest in combining with the British in their efforts.[39] In fact, the United States ambassador to France, William Sharp, wanted a large group of Americans stationed in Russia specifically to counter British economic efforts. He confessed that his interest in Russia's economic potential had begun when he learned of British companies teaching their employees Russian in expectation of future commercial opportunities there. The United States, Sharp clearly believed, should not be left behind; nor should the resource rich but technology poor Russian people be deprived of American assistance.[40]

And England was not the only Ally looking for gain. The Japanese openly tried to use intervention to expand their economic penetration of Russia. American businessmen took very definite note of this, and much of the tension in United States-Japanese relations at that time and later can be traced to this origin. As early as March 1918 one government official had opined that "if a 'new world order' is to be created at the end of this war Japan must be cast out of Siberia."[41]

Whatever war-related or altruistic reasons may have motivated the War Trade Board, or Wilson, or Redfield, or the

State Department, these same planners, plus others inside and outside government, looked at Russia as an "open door" opportunity. Someday the war would be over; but America's quest for overseas markets was unending. People like Wilson and House believed an *American* economic program could, if handled properly, accommodate a diversity of objectives none of which seemed—to them—mutually exclusive. They had less faith in Allied motivations. Reports of British and Japanese activities in Russia may well have forced Wilson's hand and precipitated September's rapid progress toward the creation of an American assistance program.

September 1918 marked a turning point in economic planning for Russia. The variety of considerations and suggestions with which Wilson had been deluged, the international variables complicating Russian policy, and the limitations of feasibility may, by then, have had time to jell into a tangible and practicable program. Wilson may simply have decided to delegate the whole matter to someone else. Whichever the case, by the end of that month he had turned over almost all responsibility for the implementation of a program to Vance McCormick and the War Trade Board.

Before that happened, however, direction and leadership of a sort materialized in the field. In early September, the United States ambassador to Japan, Roland Morris, went on a Siberian fact-finding trip to formulate recommendations on how best the United States could help the Russian people. Morris ended up spending considerable time in Siberia and was the senior American government official on the scene throughout the Russian Bureau's lifetime. As such, Morris had the unenviable task of implementing Wilson's distinctions between political interference, military intervention, and economic assistance. The president wanted it made "clear to Morris that the ideas and purposes of the Allies with respect to what should be done in Siberia . . . are ideas and purposes with which we have no sympathy." Lansing's translation of these instructions referred more specifically to military contacts and was couched more diplomatically, but the message remained the same. Neither Wilson nor

Lansing seems, however, to have been thinking in primarily economic terms at the time.[42]

In his reports, Morris did think economically, arguing that, should an inter-Allied council be formed, it not be given control over any American programs: "I think this would complicate the situation and have a tendency to hamper our influence." He believed that field representatives could work informally with the Allied agents, thereby avoiding duplication, without establishing formal ties and obligations. His projection of "informal" contacts fitted well with Lansing's "assumption" that there was no need for formal arrangements.[43]

Morris's presence in Siberia gave officials in Washington someone to whom they could refer questions and in whose answers they could have confidence. Theoretically, this link to the actual conditions in Siberia would make it easier for policy-makers to formulate realistic programs. Those same policy-makers, with little personal knowledge of Russia, also relied heavily on Ambassador Bakhmetev for "background" and suggestions. He, of course, tried to steer American policy along lines which would be most beneficial to, and realistic for, Russia.

Bakhmetev wrote two papers which appeared in late August or early September. One, on reforming Russian currency, received very positive consideration and became the core of America's currency proposals.[44] The other, a kind of commentary on and guide for economic undertakings, proved less specifically adaptable but did give its American readers some perspective on the Russian situation with which they would be dealing.[45]

The ambassador emphasized that no program could expect to mold Russia into some preconceived image, that no social stability could be forced on the people from outside, and that assistance would have to adapt itself to the course of Russia's "national consolidation." Politics should not be allowed to interfere with economics or with the process of reconstruction. The Russian people, Bakhmetev felt, would be less concerned about which government sponsored which program that about the results of the program and the benefits accruing to them. Bakhmetev tried to impress on Americans that Russia was, in fact, Russia—and not necessarily an incipient United States of Russia.[46]

Not all Russians were so emphatic on that point. Also in September 1918 the Association of Russian Engineers for Relief of Russia, located in the United States, urged Wilson to send a civil expedition to Russia which would provide the "necessary assistance to enable [the Russian people] to resist German domination" and which could educate the Russian people "to American institutions, American ideals and American sincerity." It is hard to tell whether the Russian engineers really did want to make Russia into America or whether they used that argument as a selling point to appeal to America's ego.[47]

Bakhmetev's insistence in pointing up Russia's particular needs may be partly explained by his recognition of the magnitude of Russia's problems. The ambassador, for example, did not think any program could even get started until reliable transportation and communication systems were available; his American readers may have had trouble conceptualizing the full extent of the disruption of such services, never comparable to those in the United States under the best of circumstances. Bakhmetev echoed a point made earlier by the War Trade Board: the current difficulty in redistributing goods was as much a problem as the stoppage of imports. Given these conditions, it followed that a commercial mission alone would not be enough. Russia needed help across a broad economic spectrum.[48]

Whatever the size and nature of any American economic program in Russia, it would need a home office located in Washington. The Russian Bureau records contain an unsigned, but probably War Trade Board, memorandum ascribable to late August or early September on the need for a clearing house in the United States for information on Russian economic conditions. The absence of such a central office was creating problems. All kinds of information accumulated in various government offices, but, because it was not being coordinated, collated, or analyzed at any central point, this information was often incomplete, unavailable, or ignored. American businessmen wanted someplace to come to discuss Russian-related ideas and problems. There was now no one logical government office for them to go to. All in all, lack of centralization was creating an unfortunate impression of chaos or unconcern both at home and abroad and, to say the least, a duplication of labor. The memorandum went on to suggest that the War Trade Board take on the responsibility of centralizing activities. It incorporated representatives from all other government departments interested in Russia; it had the personnel and experience to handle the work; and, since any economic transactions with Russia involved licensing by the board, it was, more than any other department at the present time, "forced to deal with practical aspects of the Russian economic situation."[49]

The State Department was thinking in similar but even more inclusive terms. Breckinridge Long wanted centralization under one person, who could supervise, control, and coordinate all those "civil, political, military and humanitarian" activities in Russia currently being administered by a variety of government agencies. He thought the present arrangement could only result in "confusion and lack of accomplishment." On August 29, Lansing seconded Long's suggestion.[50]

There were, therefore, two ideas under consideration: one involved an economic mission to Russia; the other, an agency to coordinate Russian-related activity and information. It was not until these two ideas met and married that America's economic program for revolutionary Russia began to take tangible shape.

The first step in that direction may have been a September 9 letter from Lansing to Wilson, drafted by Auchincloss. The Czechoslovak troops in Russia needed supplies. If the United States planned to provide them, it had to do so quickly. And, the secretary wondered, might not such an effort be expanded to encompass a larger relief program? The State Department tried to goad Wilson into action by suggesting that "It is to you that liberal opinion throughout the world is looking for a sound, constructive plan for assisting Russia." For the first time, the State Department openly advocated that Vance McCormick be appointed to head the program and that the War Trade Board be its parent agency. The desire for action had taken precedence over interdepartmental rivalries. Auchincloss was not "terribly hopeful that the President will do anything about" these suggestions, but his pessimism was only partly warranted. By September 12 Wilson had assigned Bernard Baruch of the War Industries Board, Vance McCormick of the War Trade Board, and Edward Hurley of the Shipping Board to "actively cooperate to see that the necessary supplies got off to [the Czechoslovaks in] Russia at the earliest possible time." Auchincloss liked what he interpreted as a transfer of initiative away from the Commerce Department. But this proposal was only a partial measure, aimed primarily at the Czechoslovaks, and as of September 19 he did not know whether anything further would be done.[51]

As it turned out, the problems inherent in supplying the Czechoslovaks did focus attention on a larger-scale Russian supply operation. One War Trade Board planner expressed fear that, unless the same supplies sent to the Czechoslovaks were made available to the local Russian population, either the Russians would forcibly appropriate the Czechoslovak supplies for themselves or the inequities would create jealousy and ill feeling. To avoid this, he suggested that the board send out field representatives to determine the most urgent needs among the relevant Russian population. Then, under the tightest of licensing controls, qualifying American exporters would be allowed to ship specifically designated goods into those target populations. Once in Russia, the goods would be under the complete control of the board's field representatives. It was assumed that Russia's cooperative societies would be the primary recipients.[52] It was also assumed that those same cooperatives would be allowed to export to the United States in order to establish credits to pay for their purchases. In his wrap-up paragraph the author conceded that "it is admittedly a provisional plan only" which might in the near future be transformed by the creation of an "international corporation for trade with Russia without profit." This was but one of many plans written to be implemented unilaterally but with the ever present possibility of internationalization. It was also the skeleton outline of what would in fact become the Russian Bureau.[53]

But first, Wilson had to be divested of his Commerce Department orientation. Working together now, McCormick and Auchincloss agreed that any program would be difficult, particularly since Redfield had "messed the matter up to such an extent that it is almost impossible to get it straight." Wilson seems to have concurred, rather belatedly, in this appraisal. He told House that Redfield's activities in previous months had made it "impossible" to go ahead with an economic and relief policy for Russia. It is not clear from the record just exactly how "the matter" had been "messed up" or whether Redfield was really to blame. There is no reason to believe either McCormick or Auchincloss knew of Wilson's role in the "mess up" and so their disdain is understandable. Wilson's willingness to blame Redfield for his own ideas and/or his own indecision would seem a little callous. In any case, having now taken the matter out of Redfield's hands and given it to the War Trade Board, Wilson "hoped something would come of it."[54]

Something did. In late September Wilson, in Gordon Auchincloss's words, gave Vance McCormick and the War Trade Board "complete charge of the Russian situation so far as economic relief is concerned." Auchincloss was delighted: "We made more progress in connection with Russian matters this afternoon than has been made during the last six months." The progress included both an economic relief effort and a centralizing agency in Washington.[55]

While the need to send supplies to the Czechoslovak Legion obviously precipitated a crystalization of economic relief efforts, the Russian Bureau was not created primarily to facilitate that supply effort. Plans for a relief program had long been in the works, but Wilson had difficulty accepting any which involved significant government, as well as private sector, participation. But he agreed to government responsibility for the Czechoslovak supplies. The unidentified author of the argument that aid to Russians would prevent friction with the Legion succeeded, finally, in convincing Wilson to accept government participation in the relief program as well. The record is unclear on whether this was the result of a conscious effort to break the logjam of presidential single-mindedness or a happy, unplanned twist of fate.

Ironically, all the progress toward Russian relief spelled the end of House's, Auchincloss's, and the State Department's involvement. Along with a new agency there emerged a new group of people to deal with Russian economics. Most of the early planners left center stage. New, relatively unknown—at least in diplomatic circles—administrators and experts brought into the wartime regulatory agencies assumed responsibilities for economic relief in Russia. Few of these people were high ranking and few left records. Many of their personalities remain obscure although hints can sometimes be glimpsed from the language and substance of their communiqués.

Vance McCormick created an agency officially called the War Trade Board of the U.S. Russian Bureau, Incorporated. Established under the authority of the War Trade Board and therefore limited in life to that of the parent agency, the Russian Bureau was a public corporation with an authorized capital of $5 million, all of which was subscribed by the United States government. The certificate of incorporation, as was common at that time, spelled out every imaginable commercial, financial, and agricultural activity as legitimate corporate activity "in any part of the world."[56]

The most concise picture of the bureau's plan of operation appears in the instructions sent to the Russian Bureau's newly appointed field representative in Siberia. Drafted by McCormick's assistant, John Foster Dulles, this Cable #1 announced that President Wilson had approved a "provisional plan for rendering economic aid to Russia" through the licensed export of needed supplies to Siberia and other areas. Licensing at home and distribution and sale in Russia would all be under the control of the War Trade Board and, more specifically, its subsidiary, the Russian Bureau. Here in capsule form was the corporate commercial goal of the Russian Bureau.[57]

The goods to be sold to Russia would originate from two sources: private capital, and the $5 million fund available to the bureau to supplement private capital resources. An estimate of the "character and amount" of goods available in America for trade would be (and in fact was) obtained through the processing of applications for export licenses submitted by interested companies. Decisions on which licenses to grant would be made in consultation with the field manager, who would also exercise "effective control of the manner, place and terms" of all resulting transactions.[58]

The terms of American-Russian trade were to be "equitable." While profit was perfectly acceptable, "no grounds should be provided for charges of exploitation." Goods should reach those Russians who most needed them, but, in order to avoid "great jealousy and ill feeling" if the Czechoslovaks had goods not available to the local population, priority was to be given to accommodating those particular Russian shortages. Ideally, Russian-American trade (i.e., Russian goods imported into the United States) would concentrate on items which "might otherwise become available to the enemy" or which were "needed" in the United States. Cooperative societies appeared the most likely customers and suppliers; dealing with them would also make the transactions easier to monitor.[59]

So far, Cable #1 had described bureau operations primarily as a go-between for American private interests and Russian consumers. In addition, the bureau could, on its own account and using its revolving capital fund, buy, ship, and sell commodities needed in Russia which, for one reason or another, did not find interested private sector dealers. The government money could also be used by the field manager to buy emergency supplies available locally or in Japan or China. But the public funds would not, under normal circumstances, compete with or take profits away from the private sector.[60]

Since there was a war on and the government controlled all shipping space and had concentrated it in the Atlantic trade routes, transportation of supplies to and from Russia presented a problem. The bureau hoped to secure at least 15,000 tons of shipping space per month, but much of this would be needed to deliver Czechoslovak supplies and railroad material to Colonel Stevens and his Russian Railway Service Corps—both of which had a more immediate relation to the war effort than did the equally important, but longer-term Siberian economy. (One of the bureaucratic, if not corporate, realities of the Russian Bureau was that it facilitated other American operations in Russia for which it had itself no direct responsibility. Using bureau shipping space allocations for Czechoslovak and railroad supplies are cases in point.) Relief and commercial shipments would have to be worked in after accommodating the higher priorities. In line with this, the field manager was to keep himself informed on all American activities in Russia, to assist them in any way possible. The field offices would, ideally, coordinate and monitor all American relief efforts and not just the bureau's.[61]

Those offices would need a variety of personnel. The War Trade Board had already dispatched one employee, "familiar with its organization and operation," to Siberia. The field manager there would have to determine his other office needs, but he had the authority "to select and dispatch to the important centers of population west along the railroad as far as conditions warrant, suitable Americans, speaking Russian if possible, whose duty it will be to investigate and report to you upon local needs and the reliability of local purchasing bodies." These persons would also ascertain the character and amount of "local products which may be made available for the use of the Armies or of civilians in other places or for export from Russia."[62]

Supplying the needs of a 7,000 man American army contingent could provide Russians with some of the foreign exchange needed to buy American goods. But generally speaking, financing, at the Russian end, was going to be awkward, especially given the unstable ruble. The United States government agreed, selectively, to grant licenses allowing "cooperative societies or other responsible persons" to export certain goods to the United States as a means of establishing credits for use in the purchase of American goods. The amount of such Russian exports would be restricted to the return cargo space available on ships that had carried goods out to Russia, "provided this quantity . . . will suffice to meet essential political and exchange requirements."[63]

Cable #1 laid out the basic rules and regulations by which the Siberian field office of the Russian Bureau was to be run. It was referred to as explanation and justification for taking or not taking actions. When an office opened in northern Russia, the field manager there simply got a copy of the Siberian cable.

A few points should be made about Cable #1. First of all, it spelled out the *projected* operations of the bureau field offices, and it envisioned fairly large-scale activities necessitating a significant number of staff operating over large areas of Russia and handling rather sizable transactions. Actual conditions in the field might not always allow for implementation of all the projections. Secondly, it seems clear that the bureau was to function as a relief program in and of itself but *also* as a coordinator and facilitator for other American activities—some of which would, in the beginning at least, have higher priorities.

The Allies did not get a copy of Cable #1. Instead they received a very vague *aide-mémoire* explaining American intentions but giving little data on the actual plan of operations. Sent out by the State Department on October 10, it leaned heavily toward moralistic platitudes and humanitarian hints aimed at deterring avarice in Americans and Allies alike. It reminded the Allies that, without embarrassing any military operations, the United States wanted "to take advantage of the earliest opportunity to relieve in some measure the immediate economic necessities of the people of Russia." Those people had to be protected "against selfish aggressive trade practices"—an objective which could not be left to the discretion of private merchants. The United States government, therefore, proposed "to permit its merchants to trade with Russia only under such direction on its part as will insure the Russian people absolute fair dealing and complete protection against exploitation and profiteering." The Allies learned that the program would have two geographic focuses: Siberia and northern Russia, both of which were, at the time, free of Bolshevik control and occupied by interventionist forces. The United States government hoped that "If and when communication between [the two regions] . . . is established," there could be a linkup between the branches both as relief programs and as activities that could be easily taken over by a future Russian government. It also hoped the Allied governments would assist in these undertakings. The War Trade Board representatives in Europe had already shown that they could cooperate "closely and harmoniously" with the Allies on questions of export and import controls and the same was expected for Russia.[64]

The Allies learned that the Russian Bureau had its own funds to fill needs which, for whatever reasons, private merchants would not satisfy. The bureau might also help establish a medium of exchange to "facilitate" both its own and private commercial transactions. In spite of obvious difficulties and recognizing that any plan would have to be modified to meet unpredictable practical conditions, the United States government felt that "the plan of action it has, after much consideration, decided upon for itself will allow it effectively to carry out its repeatedly avowed policy of serving the Russian people."[65]

Nowhere in Cable #1 or in the *aide-mémoire* was there any mention of Bolsheviks or Bolshevism. In fact, there is no evidence to suggest that anti-Bolshevik sentiment motivated creation of the Russian Bureau. In the early months of Lenin's regime very few Americans expected it to survive. The bureau's creators expected to help the totality of Russia. They did not limit their goals to that of countering one irritating but rather temporary blight on the Russian body politic.

It took Woodrow Wilson a long time to start helping the Russians help themselves. Advocates of relief efforts had had to overcome, among other things, bureaucratic rivalries and presidential uncertainty about the nature of such efforts and of government participation therein. But in spite of that delay, the ideas expressed in the Russian embassy's December 1917 memorandum had, by October 1918, been transformed into concrete plans for an American economic relief program in Russia. Those plans did not encompass all the suggestions made, at one time or another, for America's role in furthering a progressive Russia. It remained to be seen whether the Russian Bureau could or would accomplish even the goals it had set for itself, much less the wide range of expectations that many of the contributors to its creation had had in mind.

THREE

Operations and Obstacles

Once responsibility passed to the War Trade Board, creation of an economic relief agency followed quickly. Field offices opened in Vladivostok and Archangel; a multidivisional home office opened in Washington. The two obstacles plaguing Russian Bureau operations from the beginning—Russia's transportation and currency—exceeded the bureau's scope of endeavor and, consequently, kept unresolved the question of how much inter-Allied cooperation would materialize in Russia.

The Washington office of the Russian Bureau was clearly a child of McCormick's War Trade Board. Most of the corporation's board of directors and staff were simply reshuffled War Trade personnel. The board paid bureau salaries and expenses, although it later received reimbursement from bureau funds. The bureau's two original executive officers both held War Trade Board and bureau posts simulta-

neously: McCormick served as War Trade Board chairman
and bureau president; Captain H. B. Van Sinderin was War
Trade Board Director of Export-Import Licensing Division
and bureau manager. John Foster Dulles and Clarence
Woolley, the corporation's secretary and vice-president re-
spectively, also functioned in other War Trade Board capaci-
ties. The bureau's board of directors represented at least six
other government agencies or departments.[1]

McCormick functioned as the chief policy-maker, seconded by Clarence Woolley in McCormick's absence. The
Washington office manager supervised a total of eight divi-
sions: executive, exports, imports, transportation, finance,
economic intelligence and reports, personnel, and commodities investigation. It is very difficult to draw clear lines of
distinction between the bureau's corporate and bureaucratic
responsibilities. According to its corporate charter, the bureau had two primary functions: to facilitate private commercial intercourse between Russia and the United States
and, where deemed advisable, to provide on a modest scale
direct economic relief financed by the bureau itself. But the
manager's job was to oversee the conduct of "all routine
matters" and *anything else* "as may from time to time be
assigned" by the corporate officers. The entire War Trade
Board cleared any licensing relating to Russia through the
bureau, allowing it to control the flow of authorized commerce and guarantee its "desirability." As an additional
check, no licenses were issued without recommendations
from the field managers.[2]

As a first step in encouraging private sector trade, the
bureau issued a series of press notices acquainting the
American business community with the agency. It announced that export licenses to Russia (which had been suspended earlier in 1918 when the blockade of the Central
Powers had been expanded to include Russia) were again
being considered, and it requested information on what commodities might be available for such trade. The firms responding positively ranged from thread manufacturers to
International Harvester and gave the Washington office an

extensive reference list of and correspondence file with interested companies. Once lines of communication opened, the bureau helped deliver sample goods (sometimes purchased at its own expense)—primarily to Vladivostok—and kept the firms apprised of relevant developments.[3]

The bureau facilitated trade by, on occasion, providing (and charging for) shipping space. By December 1918 five ships under joint Russian Bureau-Shipping Board control had cleared port for Russia with bureau-facilitated goods on board. Although the bureau ships could not satisfy all of the demand for space, they did ease some of the shipping-related transportation problems.[4]

The financing of large scale Russian purchases raised other problems. At the bureau's behest the United States government encouraged a certain amount of Russian imports into the United States as a means of accumulating the credits Russians needed to purchase American goods. The bureau issued press notices on commodities available for import and held meetings with interested American buyers. In at least one case, Russian cooperative societies received special permission to sell a large quantity of furs to Americans, even though furs were not included on the War Trade Board's list of desirable imports. But even by making such exceptions, the United States could not assume that Russia had enough exportable goods to pay for its import needs without interim credit arrangements.[5]

Since expanded trade relations would constitute the bulk of American relief, the mission-to-Russia and the clearinghouse aspects of Russian policy rather naturally merged. The bureau assumed responsibility for gathering, coordinating, and disseminating information relevant to any economic activity or opportunity in Russia. But the sheer bulk of such data, often received from private individuals, American or Russian, or from the consuls in Russia, sometimes prevented its optimal use. It also often came too late or was blatantly unreliable. As an added complication, conditions in Russia varied dramatically over time and over terrain. Consequently, in spite of extensive files replete with reports and letters and newspaper clippings, the Washington office "clearinghouse" put most of its faith in the cable reports from its "mission" field offices. Interested companies were sent as much background material as possible but must have been told of the general unreliability of much of it. In such cases, the field manager might do an on-site updated study and forward his findings directly to the prospective company.

The Washington office also functioned as an interdepartmental government clearinghouse for United States economic policy toward Russia. The establishment and maintenance of liaison with the Military Intelligence Division of the General Staff of the Department of the Army and with the Economic Intelligence Section of the Department of State Foreign Trade Advisor's Office—both listed in the December 1, 1918, operating report as examples of progress toward cooperation with other departments—helped support the bureau's own assessment that the coordination of all government activities "in dealing with the Russian situation" was second in importance only to the relief services to be rendered.[6]

Even if not one single commercial transaction had resulted from the Russian Bureau's efforts, it would still have provided a valuable service by bringing some centralization and coordination to widely diverse operations in Washington and in the field. Members of the board of directors provided "direct contact" with the State, Treasury, and Commerce departments, the War Industries, War Trade, and Shipping boards, and the Food Administration. Ambassador Morris, Colonel Stevens of the Russian Railway Service Corps, Dr. Teusler of the Red Cross, and General Graves of the Siberian Expeditionary Force all remained in close contact with August Heid, the bureau's field manager in Siberia. Felix Cole, Heid's counterpart in northern Russia and already experienced as a United States consul, kept in touch with American, Russian, and British officials there. Ironically, the two field offices had virtually no contact with each other because of communication difficulties.[7]

The Russian Bureau had the potential to become the focal point for a variety of extensive and complex economic activities in Russia. Once established, the bureau quite naturally assumed additional responsibilities. Programs started under the auspices of other government agencies but relating to Russia now gravitated toward it.

Ambassador David Francis had been authorized to spend up to $6 million in the purchase of vital war materials in Russia. He had not, as of his departure from Russia in late 1918, spent all this money. In November President Wilson authorized turning over the cash remains of this "Francis Fund" to the Russian Bureau.[8]

The Murmansk Fund relief program in northern Russia is another case in point. England, France, and the United State agreed, also in November 1918, to send food relief to the anti-Bolshevik government established in northern Russia. Each country contributed $5 million to a common "Murmansk Fund" for the purchase of supplies for a region which had been cut off from Russia's food producing centers. In December 1918 the Russian Bureau took over administration of the Murmansk Fund. That would seem to be the primary reason for opening a bureau office in northern Russia and will be discussed in more detail later in this chapter.[9]

The task of cooperating with other American programs in Russia added military, political, and humanitarian interests to the original commercial fields of bureau concern. For example, the bureau helped facilitate shipments to the Czechoslovak troops, although the funding for that project came from a different source.[10]

The War Trade Board's Russian Bureau thus had as a corporate entity rather clearly defined, primarily commercial fields of operation, but as a government bureaucracy, especially a wartime bureaucracy, it assumed many other functions. Much the same multiplicity of tasks emerged in the field offices as well as in Washington.

August Heid, formerly the managing director of Cyrus McCormick's International Harvester operation in Siberia, became the Russian Bureau's field manager in Vladivostok. Heid knew the economic conditions and needs of Siberia and the Russian Far East. His appointment must have had the full backing of both Cyrus McCormick, who definitely had access to government decision-makers, and Ambassador Roland Morris, who was in a position to veto the appointment but instead urged Washington to centralize as much power and responsibility in Heid's office as possible. Like most Americans, Heid was anti-Bolshevik, but he retained a greater sense of proportion than did many of the State Department's consular staff in the field.[11] During 1918 and 1919 Siberia presented a less than stable political environment. The Omsk-Kolchak government expanded its area of influence through mid-1919 and then began contracting in the face of the Red Army. Long before that, the city of Vladivostok had assumed a kind of political autonomy subject to various local authorities. Bands of Cossacks, most notably one led by Seminoff, disrupted the countryside as did the large contingent (over 70,000) of Japanese occupational forces. Consequently, Heid began his official bureau duties in an environment of political and military "flux."

Both Heid and Ambassador Morris shared doubts about the feasibility of a large-scale relief effort in the immediate future. They thought financial and transportation problems needed to be resolved first and both thought any program would need to work its way slowly into more sizable dimensions. Morris cabled Washington on October 4, 1918: "I have heard during the last two weeks many elaborate schemes for the economic development of Siberia. While some of these schemes are good, they are all impractical. Our beginning must be with experiment and we should feel our way to larger operations." He believed that it would be unwise to plan any extensive economic aid to Siberia for the coming winter. There was no major food shortage and the problems associated with currency depreciation, inadequate transportation, and uneven distribution facilities successfully blocked other kinds of activities. On the other hand, and looking ahead, Morris believed that the importation and distribution of manufactured goods, when possible, even on a moderate scale would have a beneficial effect on Siberia's economic situation and exchange rate. The first step, therefore, should be to reorganize railroad operations.[12] Until then, Morris saw little purpose in sending a large staff to the Russian Bureau office. Heid reinforced Morris's observations by noting that, in part because of the insufficient organization for distribution and the disorganized conditions of transportation facilities to the inland, he could not begin to introduce imported goods into Russia on a significant level.[13]

This apparent reluctance to encourage a large-scale economic assistance program is misleading. Neither Morris nor Heid had any way of knowing the war would end so soon. Both thought there would be time to improve transportation and to build a larger operation. Both, in other contexts, thought the United States did have an important role to play in Siberia—and then all of Russia—in bringing economic stability and prosperity. That this would also mean defeating Bolshevism was probably not uppermost on their minds in that, like almost everyone else, they saw Lenin's regime as an abhorrent aberration of limited duration and of limited geographic scope. They both must also have recognized that field offices could not by themselves solve Siberia's most pressing economic problems—transportation and currency.

Nevertheless, Heid started working right away. The Vladivostok office functioned as a mail-order branch office, displaying sample goods to interested Russian buyers. Heid himself became an agent, often with full power of attorney, for American firms with no field representatives of their own. He made direct contact with American companies, handling transactions, solving problems, and relaying information.[14]

Such services were necessary in part because, for a short time during 1918, the United States government had not allowed American companies to send representatives into Siberia. That situation changed somewhat in late October when the State Department queried Heid on the advisability of allowing "reputable" agents to go. Heid's reply, to the effect that other countries' firms had agents there and that it seemed only fair to allow Americans to do likewise, reopened direct contact between some American businesses and Russian buyers. Since licenses and shipping space still needed bureau clearances, Heid could retain control over arrangements made by such contacts. For companies unwilling to finance their own representatives, Heid remained the agent. On occasion, Heid reported that certain agents or firms were not conducting their affairs "reputably"; such evaluations may have influenced whether future licenses were granted to the companies involved.[15]

Once goods got to Russia, the bureau wanted their pricing and distribution carefully supervised to prevent profiteering and exploitation. Had the volume of trade reached significant proportions, this might have created a personnel problem. On October 21 Heid reported that the manpower necessary to create an organization "suitable to distribute and control" trade was "not available now" and that such an organization could not be "perfected" for some months to come. Without a competent organization, he feared that "only confusion will be added to already confused conditions and the object of our work will be defeated and loss of time and money incurred." He also did not take advantage of his authorization to locate Americans in the field who could serve as bureau agents and travel the country. In all probability, he was hesitant to send Americans off to gather information which could not yet be used. In any case, the transportation difficulties precluded activities much beyond his immediate area.[16]

Heid did acquire a staff. As of February 8, 1919 (perhaps the peak staff size for the Siberian office), in addition to stenographic help, the Vladivostok office had five professionals plus a code clerk and an interpreter. Some of this staff was local, at least one had come from Washington, and some came to Siberia from the War Trade Board office in Japan.[17]

As was true of the home office, the Vladivostok bureau handled more than just commercial responsibilities. Heid received instructions, among other things, "to investigate and report on matters affecting needs of Czecho-Slovacs and methods of supplying such needs." As late as May 1919 he was still coordinating Czechoslovak supply deliveries and giving advice on how to evacuate their troops. He also stayed in touch with the railroad mission and other American programs in Siberia.[18]

The Russian Bureau's field office in northern Russia opened later and was less active than Heid's in Siberia. Felix Cole, the bureau's representative there, had an office in Archangel. He had been serving as a United States consul and his bureau appointment came on top of his continuing consular duties. Russian Bureau files give no indication that Cole asked for or received additional personnel.

Conditions in northern Russia differed significantly from those in Siberia. An anti-Bolshevik local government provided a stable political and economic environment; banks continued to function and the British instituted a stable currency. Historically, Archangel was a more cosmopolitan commercial center than Vladivostok and had contacts with Europe and Scandinavia of long standing. Under the steadying influence of British occupation, northern Russians lived much as they had in the past, with food supplies, not a breakdown in commercial activities, their primary problem. The Russian Bureau did not actively seek out new commercial undertakings in the north as much as it did in Siberia. First of all, the area was under tight British control. Secondly, existing contacts obviated the need for much "promotional" activity. And icy conditions in the northern ports discouraged commerce at least until the summer thaw.

This last circumstance may have been of significance in precipitating one of Wilson's first commitments toward economic relief for Russia—the "Murmansk Fund" mentioned earlier. Secretary Lansing used climate as a prod in obtaining Wilson's approval for the joint British-French-American program which Cole spent most of his bureau time administering. The story of this program illustrates the nature of British-American "cooperation" and the environment in which Cole worked.

In mid-September 1918 Lansing reminded Wilson about the British proposal to provide winter supplies for the civilian population of the Archangel/Murmansk district. Cut off from the food producing regions of Russia by Bolshevik control of central Russia, the population depended heavily on food imports. Shipments had to leave soon in order to arrive before the ports iced over. Lansing argued that more than a simple mission of mercy was at stake: the United States ambassador to Russia, now located at Archangel, "is quite clear that the security of the military assistance offered at Archangel, and the support of the civilian population in that region, will depend upon whether the impending food shortage, approaching famine conditions, will be met by the Allies and ourselves." France, England, and the United States would each contribute $5 million. The relief was not charity, nor apparently did it need to be; the Russian recipients had money and paid cash upon receipt. As a result, the Murmansk Fund, like the bureau's own capital fund, operated as a revolving account which theoretically would replenish itself.[19]

Since Wilson had not then made any decision on other Russian relief proposals, Lansing tried to get quick action by distinguishing "this matter" from other "more general plans to aid Russia" based on the physical restrictions should any delay occur. He succeeded. Wilson's approval came back in two days. Five million dollars seemed to him a "very large sum indeed" but he reluctantly agreed that "Evidently, we shall have to 'chip in' with the British Government...."[20] Here again, as with the Francis Fund, Wilson expressed concern about the size of the sum required. It is unclear whether these reactions reflected a simple budgetary parsimony, a hesitation to commit governmental rather than private sector capital, or an uncertainty about how much financial commitment the situation in Russia warranted.

The State Department did not wait for official notification that $5 million had been credited to its account, under an appropriation entitled "National Security and Defense, Department of State, 1919 (supplies for civilian population,

Russia)," before beginning the necessary arrangements. And then in November Lansing suggested and Wilson approved the transfer of these funds and their administration to the Russian Bureau.[21]

As the American official dealing with the Murmansk program at the Russian end, Cole evidenced some distress at the manner in which it was "used" by the British. He reported that they were monopolizing all food distribution made under the agreement without even asking the Americans for advice. They were also taking all of the credit, among the local population, for providing the relief. Cole thought it "self evident that the Murmansk population should be advised of the part America is taking in supplying and distributing foodstuffs." He never did work out an acceptable solution to that problem, although efforts were made to make the operation recognizably more "cooperative" from the recipients' point of view.[22]

The situation pointed up a noticeable difference between conditions in northern Russia and those in Siberia. The British and Americans were economic competitors in both places, but in northern Russia the British were in charge. Even the American troops were under British command. The United States objected only when British activities were in blatant violation of American standards or when it seemed that the British were, not so surreptitiously, trying to insinuate themselves into a dominant economic position. For example, Ambassador Francis frowned upon the British proposal to stabilize currency in the area, not because the plan was bad, but because it would operate "to the benefit of British commerce." The War Trade Board rejected what it saw as a British attempt to profit from America's willingness to import Russian goods. The British reportedly planned to buy Russian flax and sell it to the United States. The board warned Cole that it would authorize no imports of British-owned flax. It was still willing to import flax if it were Russian-owned, since the object of such imports was to create Russian credits.[23]

Generally speaking, however, the United States took a back seat in northern Russian military, political, and economic activities, consciously leaving the British in control. It is not surprising that the Russian Bureau's activities were limited. In Siberia, on the other hand, American officials felt themselves subservient to no one and the government refused to undercut its own freedom of action. Conflicts with Japan and, less frequently, with the other Allies, never significantly impaired America's autonomy and almost never resulted in accommodation such as experienced in northern Russia.

The situation in northern Russia was also dissimilar from that in Siberia because of the proximity in the north of organized Bolshevik forces and the fluidity of the "military" lines separating Bolshevik from non-Bolshevik territory. Americans in Siberia saw a lot of soldiers, ranging from United States Army troops to roaming bands of Cossack raiders, but during 1918 and 1919 they had little direct contact with Trotsky's Red Army. Any efforts to provide "reconstructive" relief in the north had to be undertaken with the awareness that tomorrow the area might be under "enemy" control. It was in such a context that the War Trade Board ran into a conflict with the State Department.

In November 1918 the board had authorized the exportation of telephone equipment to repair phone lines in Petrograd—then in Bolshevik hands but expected soon to be "liberated." The State Department worried that such repairs might "assist the Bolshevik authorities" and requested that the authorization be canceled. Although the board finally agreed to do so, the issue sparked a discussion which prompted the board of directors, on December 5, 1918, to take the following action:

> The Chairman is requested to suggest to the Department of State that the policy of economic isolation and blockade towards those sections of Russia which are under the control of the Bolshevik authorities, is one calculated to prolong the control of the Bolshevik authorities and delay the establishment in Russia of a stable and rational political order.

The War Trade Board did not think the policy of economic strangulation a wise approach to Bolshevism; one may assume that it did not like the resultant restraints on American commerce either. Five months later, in a very belated critique of the board's position, Cole would write a bitter denunciation of all things Bolshevik and of all suggestions allowing contact with Bolsheviks. In this he showed himself more representative of the State Department than of the War Trade Board.[24]

There is no reason to believe that Wilson was personally involved in or even aware of this specific War Trade Board-State Department disagreement over the proper approach to Russia. The State Department's victory does not, therefore, reflect Wilson's own preferences. The incident does serve to illustrate one of the questions that analysts of Wilson's policy need to deal with. Was his primary goal to help the Russian people, or was it to fight Bolshevism?

The reality in northern Russia of Bolshevism as a physical force gave American policy there—at least as expressed by the State Department—a much more overtly anti-Bolshevik flavor than in Siberia. The bureau's agent in the north reflected the State Department bias. In Siberia, where evidence of radicalism was more mental than physical, and where Heid, Morris, and Graves all seem to have been more concerned with physical conditions than with ideological leanings, there was much less of a specifically anti-Bolshevik emphasis. For all three, Russia's transportation difficulties presented a much more pressing problem than its politics.

One such difficulty, the shortage of shipping space and the massive congestion that often threatened to paralyze Vladivostok, resulted, during the war, from military priority allocation of almost all available ships to the Atlantic theater. After the war, with regulations removed, the shortage continued; this time because merchants found more attractive commercial opportunities elsewhere. But far and away the more important bottleneck to Russia's economic recovery was the railway system—and most specifically the Trans-Siberian, which provided the only link between eastern and western Russia and which, in Siberia, was the only mode of bulk transportation. The Trans-Siberian had been built quickly, rather inefficiently, and with unfortunate efforts at economy. Its very light rails crushed under the weight of heavy freight cars. "In 1918, the embankments and the roadbeds were inadequate. After a heavy rain, trains ran off the track like squirrels." When the line operated, it did not connect cities; rather, it had been constructed with regard to the shortest possible mileage and most advantageous terrain rather than with regard to population centers. The Russian railroad personnel had been allowed to operate at a loss, due to government subsidies, and consequently had little incentive to achieve efficiencies of performance. According to Richard Goldhurst, the civil war had added to the line's misfortunes:

> Eight hundred and twenty-six bridges were blown up by one side or the other. At least twenty stations and fourteen water supply depots were leveled. Thousands of miles of track were blasted to pieces or bent out of shape. Monies held in reserve were soon exhausted and no revenues came in.

An American journalist traveling in non-Bolshevik territories reported that no conductor had ever asked for his ticket, which was clearly not the way to guarantee a profit.[25]

Operation was further complicated by the need to obtain a ready coal supply, and the major Siberian mines experienced periodic strikes throughout the civil war period. In addition, as a consequence of its obvious value to whoever could hold it, the line became a prize for all parties to the civil war and general turmoil.

The implications of the Trans-Siberian's difficulties, for any relief efforts, were obvious. According to Ambassador Bakhmetev, no program could be effective until "reliable transportation and communication service is installed." Heid told the home office that "Transportation is key to the problem of supplying economic aid to Russia."[26]

Two early State Department memoranda on the nonmilitary facets of intervention both stressed the importance of transportation and most specifically railroads. The June 5, 1918, War Trade Board recommendations for providing aid cited the need for transportation experts and for an organization capable of handling distribution. Ambassador Bakhmetev's plan, submitted by September 1918, suggested that the lack of transportation was exacerbating the already bad conditions and that any program would need to come to grips with that situation: ". . . famine and misery are greatly indebted to the disorganization of the transportation system; grain, foodstuffs, and fuel being abundant in certain regions while entirely deficient in others." A relief program would have to provide commodities not available inside Russia and also assist with the redistribution of goods that were available but unevenly so.[27]

American interest in the Russian railway system predated both the Bolshevik revolution and plans for economic assistance programs. Under the direction of Colonel John Stevens, the Russian Railway Service Corps combined experts and technicians sent to Russia, at the Provisional Government's request, to help coordinate and improve the operations of the Trans-Siberian. The railroad, an important supply line in the war effort, suffered from general inefficiency, a chronic shortage of equipment, and a dearth of qualified personnel. The Corps would provide personnel and, it was hoped, facilitate determination and delivery of priority equipment needs.[28]

Stevens's orders specified that he was to be responsible to Russia and was to conduct his operation for the benefit of Russia. On May 31, 1917, President Wilson told Lansing that the Corps was "to report nothing back to us. They are delegated to do nothing but serve Russia on the ground, if she wishes to use them, as I understand she does." In spite of these sentiments, Stevens's presence on the Russian railways did work to America's advantage even when the line's role in Russia's war effort is discounted. Most immediately, the railroad's requirements produced orders for American equipment and machinery. More generally, a smoothly run transportation system was integral to Russia's economy, present and future, and the United States government believed America had a stake in that economy.[29]

The confusion following the Bolshevik takeover brought a temporary halt to Corps operations, but they resumed in early 1918 on those sections of the Trans-Siberian and the Chinese Eastern railways outside Bolshevik control. Though there was now no recognized Russian government to which Stevens could report, he continued to see himself as an agent of Russia and, like Wilson, viewed the mission as responsible to the best interests of the Russian people.[30] Since both Wilson and Stevens also believed that expanded trade with the United States would be to Russia's advantage, they saw no conflict of interests.

Intervention expanded American interest in Russia's transportation network. President Wilson had agreed to participate only within narrow operational confines. The American troops were there: (1) to give assistance to the Czechoslovak legion—"guard the line of communication of the Czecho-Slovaks"—presumably winding its way toward Vladivostok and thence out of Russia; and (2) to guard the huge supply depots along the railroad and in Russia's ports and keep Vladivostok open as a point of egress for the Czechoslovaks. Unfortunately, when Graves and his troops arrived they discovered that the Czechoslovaks, far from proceeding eastward expeditiously, had actively involved themselves in the Russian civil war. As a result, maintaining the railroad in order to facilitate their evacuation actually meant helping the Czechoslovaks fight the Bolsheviks.[31]

All of the Russian factions and several of the Allies were willing to fight over the Trans-Siberian. It became the focus of much international friction at the very same time that intervention participants publicly agreed on the need to co-operate on maintaining the line. It also became, with each passing day, a transportation system on the verge of total collapse after years of neglect, equipment failure, and machinery fatigue. It was in this environment that Stevens and his team operated and that the Russian Bureau began its efforts to facilitate economic relief.

Ironically, the cost of building and maintaining the Trans-Siberian had, at one time, contributed to another problem plaguing efforts at commercial relief efforts: ruble inflation and instability.[32] The Russian ruble had first assumed significance for American policy-makers when the Bolshevik takeover withdrew legitimacy from the currency internationally by depriving Russia of a recognized government. The strain of inflated wartime prices and of "printing press fever" had already greatly devalued the ruble. Then the Bolshevik revolution produced mass confusion in Russian financial circles. By 1918 there was very little faith in the ruble anywhere. All of this would make it difficult to entice American businessmen into a ruble market and suggested the need to do something to arrive at a stable medium of exchange in Russia. The anti-Bolshevik forces would also be better able to attract foreign and domestic support if they controlled a stable currency. Equally worrisome from another perspective, the Bolsheviks and Germans both controlled huge quantities of rubles. Stabilizing the existing currency would provide just that much more money by which either could finance their "nefarious" operations. Taking all of these conditions into account, Gordon Auchincloss was not alone in believing that "the only sensible way to act is to drive the rouble out of existence and to substitute for it some [other, stable] obligation."[33]

Because of the obvious problems of dealing in rubles, early 1918 references to commercial transactions with non-Bolshevik Russia assumed a barter system of exchange. But there were clear limits to barter financing if and when a sizable volume of trade was undertaken. Basil Miles, at the State Department, contemplated the use of financial experts to "help untangle the industrial and financial chaos produced by the Bolsheviks," especially including "measures to finance exchanges of commodities" between Russia and the Allies.[34]

As the interest in an economic program for Russia intensified, American policy-makers came increasingly to believe that Russia's currency problem could only be solved by the issuance of a new medium of exchange. In late August 1918 Ambassador Bakhmetev outlined a plan which became the basis for most American currency proposals. He reasoned that some form of currency would be needed to meet the intervention forces' in-country expenses and, even more to the point, a currency would be needed in conjunction with the plans for economic assistance and Russia's overall economic recovery. But, the ambassador stressed, nothing should be done that would "cause embarrassment to the future National Government of Russia in the coming task of consolidating and stabilizing the monetary system of the country." Bakhmetev put Russian interests in the forefront of his proposals and tried to steer currency reform in the direction least damaging to a future government.[35]

So many problems hampered any attempt to stabilize the existing ruble that Bakhmetev rejected the possibility. One alternative, Allied use of foreign currencies instead of rubles, would be "embarrassing . . . on account of the illiteracy of the population and its unfamiliarity with foreign specie and denominations." It would also create problems when a future government tried to reestablish a truly Russian currency.[36]

The issuance of special certificates in ruble denominations for use by Allied troops and traders offered the best approach. They would not solve Russia's broader financial problems and their quantity should be limited "to the practical needs of economic assistance and corresponding to the actual demand of exchange media." But Bakhmetev believed that the "relative value and purchasing power" of such certificates could "easily be rendered stable" relative to the commodities they purchased, that the population could understand their values, that they could be controlled to preclude benefiting Germany, and that they could easily be convertible for a future government.[37]

Even with such certificates, Russia would need, initially, so many more imports than it could pay for with exports or cash (of whatever kind) that a financial institution would be needed that could grant interim credits to pay for the imports. Stock in the kind of banking institution Bakhmetev proposed would be formed primarily through subscription by foreign governments but could also attract some private capital. Part of the stock would be converted into foreign currencies; part would be issued as bank notes, or certificates. Credits would be available for organizations engaged in commercial transactions in Russia. The participating governments could use the notes to pay the in-country expenses of their forces; merchants could use them to buy or sell goods. To prevent the notes from becoming a German source of foreign currency and to insure the stability of their value and prevent them from entering the world exchange markets, redemption into foreign currency would be permitted "only after proper consideration of each particular case."[38]

Although insisting that the bank certificates should never be regarded as Russian legal tender, Bakhmetev recognized that they might end up circulating among the Russian populace and might even come to be accepted "parallel to present currency, in payment of taxes" and other monetary obligations inside Russia. But since a future government would be able, through "proper agreement with the Allies," to assume control of the bank and withdraw the notes from circulation in exchange for a fair value of its own currency, he did not see this as a liability.[39]

Bakhmetev wanted all the participating Allies to use identical and uniform certificates, rather than each Ally establishing its own bank and its own certificates—to the multiple confusion of their users. Secretary of State Lansing, who thought little or no economic assistance would be possible until the currency problem had been solved, agreed. On September 21, 1918, after consulting with the Treasury Department and the War Trade Board, he told Wilson that some uniform inter-Allied "scheme" of currency should be devised for use throughout non-Bolshevik Russia. Uncoordinated action, with each country pursuing its own approach, would be harmful to the ruble, confusing to the populace, and embarrassing to a future Russian government. Since Lansing usually objected to inter-Allied projects, his willingness to make an exception here indicates the importance he placed on currency stabilization[40]

Lansing noted that some of the Allies had already begun individualistic approaches. The Japanese were issuing a currency redeemable in yen and were, apparently, trying to introduce the yen itself in the Siberian economy. The British were establishing a new ruble currency in northern Russia "backed in part by sterling deposits carried in London." If these alternatives proved acceptable to the local populations, they would give Japan and England significant commercial advantage and economic influence in their respective areas of occupation. The creation of a uniform Allied currency would undercut these nationalistic efforts— which Lansing saw as injurious both to Russia and to American opportunities in Russia.[41]

While there are some indications that American currency planners saw their proposals as anti-Bolshevik, the bulk of the evidence suggests that the immediate goals of currency reform during 1918 were either directed against Germany or seen as a way to facilitate trade and, thus, relief. The problem with each interventionist nation establishing a full-scale alternate currency of international acceptability (i.e., the yen, or sterling backed rubles) was that this would portend the division of Russia into fiscally divorced regions which it would be difficult for a Russian government to reunite under its own financial sovereignty. A sweeping, joint currency reform program would, on the other hand, have obvious political (and anti-Bolshevik) ramifications, which seemed very much like interference in Russia's internal affairs.

Wilson must have been torn. He had already made it bluntly clear that the United States did not intend to cooperate with the Allies in any projected political undertakings. Economic exploitation of Russia was equally distasteful. Cooperation in arriving at a uniform stable currency might make it that much easier for unscrupulous interference and exploitation—whether economic or political. Noncooperation would simply give Japan and England a completely free hand in their respective areas of influence.

The Treasury Department queried currency reform ideas —but for different reasons. It worried about legalities and logistics and rejected out of hand one suggestion that a new currency be backed by outstanding Russian government bonds, arguing that there was no recognized Russian government to give legitimacy to the bond obligations. (The United States government might be giving continued recognition to the defunct Provisional Government; a more practical Treasury Department was not about to let that rather ethereal government assume new, unsupported financial responsibilities.) Believing that any new currency should be backed by commodities "so that its purchasing power could be demonstrated" to the local population, Treasury officials found the Russian ambassador's plan much preferable to the British. But if there was any chance the introduction of a new circulating medium was going to be only a "temporary expedient" or would not be accepted by the Russians, the Treasury Department wanted Americans in Russia to continue using the present ruble.[42]

In spite of his own doubts and those of the Treasury Department, Wilson did approve a currency plan in early October which argued that "while transactions will doubtless partake of the nature of barter, a direct exchange of commodities will generally be impracticable, and some medium must be provided to facilitate purchases and sales and to permit of that distribution of imported commodities which is desirable." According to this proposal, a public corporation similar to the Russian Bureau itself would be formed to oversee such currency, which would be issued in amounts (initially) corresponding to the capital appropriated to the Murmansk Fund and to the Russian Bureau, i.e., $10 million, and whatever private capital, put on deposit with the War Trade Board, might be attracted to the Russian trade. Since the dollar amounts corresponded to America's investment in Russia, this was clearly a unilateral currency reform framework. But it could be altered to accommodate an inter-Allied program.[43]

Currency planners outside the Russian Bureau assumed that each of the Allies would create a similar corporation and that "these national institutions should act only through a joint agency or council so that any currency issued would be issued by the banks jointly and in the name of all." Theoretically, such a creation "would promote a full disclosure by each government of its financial and economic purposes in Russia." American policy-makers had been reimpressed with the reality of commercial rivalry over Russia by reports of Japanese activities in Siberia and by Ambassador Francis's report in October that the British currency plan for northern Russia "will inure to the benefit of British commerce." But the *aide-mémoire* through which the Allies were informed of the public corporation idea did not include any references to "full disclosure." Nor did it insist upon the creation of a joint agency, but simply suggested that the various national currency agencies, once established, confer with each other. Ideally, "it would be through the instrumentality of such allied representatives that any issue of a medium of exchange or currency could be made."[44]

While all of this suggests that most American currency planners thought in terms of a cooperative effort that would produce a uniform currency, progress toward that goal was not immediate, in spite of the president's approval of one plan. Wilson still believed that the Allies had ulterior motives and he was not going to be rushed into a currency program that would aid and abet their purposes.

Once the Russian Bureau was established, its financial expert, L. K. Thorne, took an active part in discussions and analyses of the various currency plans in circulation. He became, as it were, a kind of simultaneous clearinghouse and critic, and he did not always agree with earlier or other groups of currency planners. In October 1918 Vance McCormick made it clear that the Russian Bureau economic relief plans did not now include any joint programs, even though the government apparently did hope the Allies would initiate similar unilateral programs which might be mergeable at some later date. When the British, who had gone ahead and instituted their sterling-backed rubles, asked whether the United States wanted to join them in a similar program in Siberia, the bureau directors decided to defer action in order to give their own personnel time to evaluate the currency situation.[45]

On November 7, 1918, Thorne submitted a summary and analysis of French, British, and American currency proposals. While the American plan envisioned currency issued "against commodities imported in Russia," a French plan suggested currency issued against Allied treasury warrants in the amount of their military expenses, Allied loans to Russian district governments, and "documentary bills of exchange" to be signed by several persons, at least one of whom must be a non-Russian. The British plan was similar to that already in use in northern Russia: currency would be issued in exchange for sterling in London, in exchange for old ruble notes at some fixed price, and in exchange for a limited amount of Provisional Government treasury bills. Thorne found the American plan too limited to accommodate actual currency needs. He thought all the proposals would encounter problems in redemption and conversion.[46]

Nevertheless, on November 15, Treasury Department, State Department, and War Trade Board representatives approved plans for an "international rouble note," to be issued through a joint agency, and which would be the "joint and several obligations" of the participating countries. The plan presumed total cooperation among the parties and included the provision that any such operation should allow a future Russian government the "opportunity to assume and become responsible for the then outstanding certificates."[47]

Either as a substitute for or as a component of the "international" version, another November 15 memorandum outlined the issuance of certificates by the Russian Bureau alone. Employment of such certificates would be as extensive as possible, covering almost all facets of American involvement in Russia. This was a redrafting of the "unilateral" version of the trade certificate idea, broadened to satisfy Thorne's objections, but it was not altogether successful in so doing. Either the armistice or Thorne, or both, would block implementation of both unilateral and international plans.[48]

After the November 1918 armistice, Thorne became more critical of any plans to substitute a new currency for the old. Such a move "would impose hardship upon the masses of people who have accepted the [old] money in full confidence" and would cause a general "distrust in paper currency by the masses." Although active opposition to the Bolsheviks had by now entered into currency reform motivation, Thorne did not think a new currency would help stop the radicals and no lasting solution to Russia's currency problems could be arrived at "until a staple [stable?] government exists which cannot be tampered with."[49]

In December Thorne specifically recommended against the issuance of Russian Bureau certificates: "a consideration of the purpose which these certificates are to serve will indicate that under present conditions their issuance is unnecessary." One of those conditions was undoubtedly the armistice—which withdrew the concern about German exploitation of rubles. Another related condition may have been the presumed end of war-related activities—such as the Russian Bureau and military intervention—which had highlighted the need for currency reform. Finally, Thorne insisted that it would be just as practical, and probably a great deal less confusing, simply to establish credit relations among the parties involved in dealings in Russia. It is impossible to tell whether Thorne's were the decisive arguments, but by December 1918 currency reform planning had been suspended, pending discussions at the peace conference.[50]

Since no forward progress toward a stable currency took place during 1918, the Russian Bureau field offices had to deal with the old, inflated ruble. Heid and Ambassador Morris approached the currency program from different perspectives. Morris believed that "Unless our government cooperates with some American agency in devising a method to limit the risks at present involved in rates of exchange we cannot hardly [*sic*] expect to aid Russia by the importation of manufactured goods." On the other hand, Heid reported that workers and farmers had ample money to purchase necessities and that distribution and profiteering, not currency per se, were the primary problems—at least on his initial scale of operation. These two reports reflected a dilemma of economic aid to Russia. If undertaken on a truly significant scale, something would have to be done about the currency. Given the actual level of activity, it seemed easier to leave matters as they were and avoid complications.[51]

In either case, the establishment of an American bank branch office in Vladivostok could do no harm. Heid felt that it would draw into circulation large sums of money being hoarded by the peasants. Certainly it would facilitate commercial transactions and possibly could serve as a base for the issuance of a new currency if that course were pursued. Representatives from National City Bank went to Vladivostok in mid-November and a branch did in fact open. But a private American bank could by itself do nothing to issue a new viable currency. Nor could it significantly expand the currently feasible volume of Russian-American trade.[52]

The first shipment made to Russia aboard bureau-controlled shipping consisted of Red Cross and military supplies for the Czechoslovak troops, equipment for the railroad, and kerosene oil. Not much of this qualified as "relief" to the Russian people. A second shipment, in November 1918, included Red Cross and military supplies for the Czechoslovaks, more oil (apparently at Heid's request), military shoes, rifles, locomotives, machinery for railroad use, freight car parts, lead, and nine tons of secondhand clothes. Heid dispersed all of this, but since these two shipments accounted for most of the Vladivostok-bound tonnage allocated to the Russian Bureau in October and November, the amount of purely commercial movement—at least movement for which the bureau provided shipping space—was limited, at best.[53] There may simply not have been enough time to culminate commercial transactions. Or the higher priority given Red Cross or Czechoslovak or railroad shipments may have precluded commercial cargoes.

The arrival of such noncommercial shipments did make return cargo space available. Theoretically, Heid could have coordinated some rather extensive Russia-to-America trade even if the America-to-Russia flow was bottlenecked. However, in December Heid reported that he probably would not be able to arrange such return cargo.[54] He had discovered one of the many obstacles to such trade: the shortage of Russian goods for which there was enough need in the United States to warrant importation. The restrictions on Russian exports to the United States were just as tight as those on American exports to Russia, if not more so. While both were contingent upon available shipping space, Russian exports could be shipped *only* aboard those vessels specifically allocated for bureau use. But without such sales Russian buyers of American goods would have trouble financing their purchases. It became necessary, therefore, to make certain exceptions to the rules. As we have seen, the War Trade Board agreed to import Russian-owned flax, but it refused to import that same flax under British ownership. After some hesitation, the importation of furs, for which America had no pressing need but of which Russia had an abundance, was allowed in order to establish Russian credits. Ironically, at the same time these fur exports from Russia were approved, the committee in charge of supplying the Czechoslovak army authorized the purchase of some 20,-000 fur coats in China for shipment to Russia. This may have made better financial than logistical sense.[55]

Another problem Heid cited in developing a Russian export trade involved transportation logistics inside Russia: the difficulty of moving goods from the interior to the coast. Rail transportation ranged from unreliable to unavailable.

Heid was discovering that efforts to increase trade between America and Russia during a domestic civil war and an international world war faced at least one "vicious circle" obstruction. The railroads could not function without equipment, and economic assistance could not function without the railroads. The railroad equipment arrived (when it arrived at all) by ship, and there was very little shipping space. This shortage did not result from merchant reluctance to travel to Vladivostok, even though conditions in that port might have given some people pause. Rather, with all American shipping under tight war emergency controls, there existed an absolute shortage of vessels available for Pacific duty. This would obviously hamper trade in both directions. Early projections of the monthly tonnage allocations to the Russian Bureau for Siberian operations—relatively small to begin with—were cut back. Since the first priorities were supplies for the Czechoslovaks and the railroads, this left very little room for commercial goods. When the War Department tried to divert *all* shipping to Europe, the War Trade Board complained that such a move would "involve the frustration, for the time being, of the Board's Russian program." Competing government authorities compromised by agreeing to allocate 4,000 tons per month for War Trade Board use on army transports "plying to Vladivostok" and, in addition, to grant the board the use of "three of the vessels now in the Pacific which were least suited for trans-Atlantic service." In something of an understatement, the directors noted "that the allowance of tonnage thus secured seriously crippled the Board's Russian program since it had been contemplated that shipments amounting to approximately 25,000 tons per month would be made beginning January 1, 1919." The Washington office was probably thinking of the shipping problem when it suggested that Heid might want to secure urgently needed relief supplies in Japan or China, where transportation to Russia would be less of a problem.[56]

Heid could, if he wanted, draw on the bureau's own capital to purchase locally or in Japan or China supplies which were urgently needed in specific areas of Russia or which could not be obtained through American dealers. He turned down the opportunity to do so when he rejected the home office's October 15 suggestion that it open credits for his use in the purchase of supplies outside the United States. Apparently interpreting his rejection as a preference to buy American goods and to give as much business as possible to the private sector, Washington suggested that he reconsider.

Buying locally would make it much easier to provide necessary relief rapidly.[57]

Heid still demurred. First of all, he thought the immediately available organization (his own and the Russians') insufficient to ensure equitable distribution of goods. Further inland, where the need would be greatest, reliable transportation was difficult to obtain. In any case and in spite of some shortages, Heid thought there was little "likelihood of immediate suffering among the north Siberian population." What hardships did materialize would be among the refugees and prisoners of war, who could not afford to buy goods and who, he assumed, would be ministered to by the Red Cross. Heid also had reports that such imperative needs as did exist were being capitalized on by those individuals and groups anxious to engage in profiteering. He did not want to invest government money in large-scale commodity programs until he could accurately ascertain need and monitor distribution. He was not unalterably opposed to the establishment and use of credits; he just did not think current conditions warranted such actions. When and if those conditions changed, he would of course submit the requests for credits as suggested.[58]

When and if conditions changed, Heid did think there was a potentially good market in Russia for American products: "A large per cent of the monetary wealth here is in the hands of workmen and farmers so that no suffering should occur for lack of means to purchase commodities." And while there may have been no major food shortages in Siberia, the workers and farmers did need a wide variety of hardware, tools, implements, and machinery. It would seem that Heid saw little if any "emergency" relief needs in Siberia; but there was, he thought, a vast market for the everyday implements of life which Russians could use to enhance their condition and speed prosperity. As of late 1918 very little of this commercial potential had been realized.[59]

If wartime conditions hampered bilateral relief efforts, might there be a chance to help Russia help itself by helping it reopen its own producing facilities? The Red Cross representatives in Siberia asked whether the Russian Bureau could help reopen factories and shops currently standing idle, thus producing Russian goods for sale in Russia. Inquiries got underway. The home office cabled Heid that it was trying to get a group of textile manufacturers to send persons out to Vladivostok "to operate clothing shops under your supervision." This episode suggests that the Russian Bureau felt a commitment to helping Russia that went beyond simply selling Russia American goods. In fact, in light of this and other possible operations, the bureau thought it "desirable" for Heid to find "one Russian of unquestioned integrity who would appreciate and sympathize entirely with [America's] unselfish plan of assisting Russia ... and upon whom [Heid] could call for counsel on [related] subjects." Such a person might also be able to help avoid labor problems, the home office suggested, and if no one was available in the field, it thought it could locate a "proper man" from among the Russians resident in the United States.[60]

There is no evidence that anything further came of the clothes manufacturing idea. The American manufacturers may not have been interested; Heid may have given the idea less than enthusiastic reception; or perhaps the armistice diverted everyone's attention.

By the end of 1918 the Russian Bureau had been in existence three months. It would be unrealistic to expect any program to have achieved significant successes or failures in so short a time period. In its own end of year analysis, the bureau felt its operations had been most tangibly hobbled by the shortage of shipping space created by the diversion of almost all available transport to the European theater of war.[61] Transportation and currency problems inside Russia had imposed other obstacles to the relief effort.

Nevertheless, the Russian Bureau could look with satisfaction to a few major accomplishments and even more auspicious beginnings. The United States government had made a firm commitment to providing assistance to Russia.

The inter-Allied food relief program for northern Russia was running smoothly. The groundwork had been laid for renewed and expanded trade relations with Russia. The hope was that economic and political stability would soon follow. The bureau field managers were coordinating a variety of official and semiofficial American activities in Russia; the Washington office was beginning to establish itself as a focal point for Russian economic policy. Ironically, peace threatened to end the Russian Bureau just when it was getting started.

FOUR

The Bureau in Limbo

For most historians, and for many Americans at that time, celebration of the armistice and war's end was overshadowed by anticipation of the dramatic achievments in international peace and justice expected from the Paris peace conference. Once convened, the peacemakers concentrated on the terms of peace with Germany, the restructuring and stabilization of central and eastern Europe, the ideological international challenge of Bolshevism, and the creation of a new world order. Russia's chaos further complicated their already awesome task.[1] Not surprisingly, in the hectic months of late 1918 and early 1919, Woodrow Wilson devoted little time to consideration of the Russian Bureau's future. In fact, he made no recorded references to the bureau until it became apparent that the peace treaty would be months in the making, that the situation in Russia was not improving, and that the bureau was, on its own initiative, preparing to terminate operations.

Ironically, the armistice did little to change the original reasons for American interest in Russia's economic well-being. Germany, even in defeat, might still be able to exert undue influence over a weak and vulnerable Russian economy, whatever form of government might evolve there. Americans still saw Russia as a potential market and still worried about imperialistic and exploitative competition from both European and Asian rivals. Wilson still had hopes for the emergence of a progressive Russian polity. The only major change between late 1917 and early 1919 was an increasing concern about Bolshevism—in Russia and elsewhere—which grew in direct proportion to the decreased threat of German militarism. But many Americans believed that Bolshevism (and probably the Bolsheviks as well) would vanish with a return to peace and prosperity.

By 1919 the State Department had become more vehemently anti-Bolshevik than ever. Secretary Lansing believed Bolshevism to be "the most hideous and monstrous thing that the human mind has ever conceived." Consul Ernest Harris, in far away Siberia, feared that the American public lacked commitment to the anti-Bolshevik cause:

I am inclined to think that the American people do not fully realize what Bolshevism signifies. For fifteen months it has held European Russia in a state of terror and there are no signs that the Russian people of their own accord possess sufficient force to free themselves. . . . Bolshevism is a greater danger than the militarism, [which] at least stood for law and order while Bolshevism stands only for destruction of life and property. Bolshevism constitutes a real world danger and should be literally stamped out [. In] principle *it* knows no geographical boundaries or national units. The Allies should deal with it, not as a Russian problem but as a world problem and as the aspirations of Germany have been definitely defeated, Bolshevism, an actual menace to civilization, must be met and crushed. . . . Bolshevism is no longer a Russian problem but one which endangers all humanity.

For Woodrow Wilson, ending the threat of Bolshevism was second in importance only to establishing a league of nations which would bring justice, reason, and stability to the world. He believed that "Europe and the world cannot be at peace if Russia is not." Since it was inconceivable to him that Russia at peace might still be a Bolshevik Russia, he defined a peaceful Russia as one in which the radical influence had been, at the very least, tempered.[2]

The American delegation at Paris disagreed with the Allies on how to deal with the Bolshevik problem. Colonel House and General Bliss, in particular, felt that military action against Bolshevism inside or outside Russia would be useless. Bliss frequently said using guns against Bolshevism would be like trying to stop a flood with a broom. An army might end the Bolsheviks—but not Bolshevism.[3]

The European Allies were not so sure. At one point in the conference they contemplated sending a large military assault against Lenin's regime. The Churchillian plan failed to materialize primarily because, when pressed, none of the major Allies was willing or able to contribute enough manpower and resources to make any such effort practical. This helps explain their willingness to lend support—on a much smaller scale—to the White Russian forces trying to do the job themselves. It also helps explain why the interventionist troops already in Russia remained.[4]

The American public had never shown much enthusiasm for America's military intervention in Russia. When the war ended and the troops who had gone to Europe came home, the public was even more hostile to their continued presence in Russia. The American delegation at Paris felt these domestic pressures for withdrawal, but it encountered resistance to such a move from the Allies and from some of its own government officials. Wilson complained of the Russian situation that "it is harder to get out than it was to go in"—even though he seems clearly to have wanted out.[5]

In fact, intervention and withdrawal were more questions of Allied-American than Russian-American policy and had created friction for some time. The clash with England over military and political objectives became so acute in northern Russia that the United States had threatened to pull out even before the war ended. After the armistice, it was almost impossible to justify continued intervention for nonideological reasons. Whether or not the United States did in fact openly concur with the more blatant European desire to rid Russia of Bolsheviks, its continued military presence implied a willingness to oppose the Bolsheviks militarily.[6]

Secretary of War Newton Baker found the situation unfortunate. America's original reasons for intervention had evaporated. Baker felt that England and Japan were taking advantage of the American presence and he wanted to pull the troops out. Replying to prointervention arguments, he also did not think America "have a right to use military force to compel the reception of our relief agencies." Whether the Russian people liked the Bolsheviks or not, that was their problem. Baker wanted to "order our forces home by the first boat" and limit future aid to economic assistance. In Siberia, General Graves, commanding the Siberian Expeditionary Force, charged that interventionist support of the Omsk-Kolchak regime was prolonging the civil war, exacerbating the class tension, and unduly endangering his troops. He wanted out.[7]

Frank Polk at the State Department was among those who supported continued intervention. If the troops left, he reasoned that, among other things, the Stevens railway mission would have to leave as well. As of November 1918, the Russian Bureau's own Vance McCormick also recommended continued intervention. In fact he wanted more troops sent. In all probability, McCormick saw such troops more as a counter to the Japanese and as protection for the railroad than as a potential for military operations against the Bolsheviks. Most of the consular and embassy staff still in Russia also favored continued intervention, many of them for overtly anti-Bolshevik reasons.[8]

President Wilson's inability to follow Graves's and Baker's advice did not mean he concurred with the anti-Bolshevik advocates, or even with Polk and McCormick. Nor did it mean he connected a military presence with continued economic assistance. Wilson wanted to write a peace treaty that would bring about the best of all possible worlds. Russia was vital to his ultimate success, but so too was the cooperation of the other major world powers; and little could be done about Russia without such cooperation. In trying to resolve the Russian component of his broader world plan, Wilson set himself a very difficult task. Nevertheless, he hoped international compatibility of purpose would be possible, and the administration announced soon after the armistice that no new actions would be taken and no new policy decisions made until after the president had met with the others in Paris to work out joint policy decisions. Since those decisions might conceivably need military support, the troops should not be withdrawn until the decisions had been made. Wilson might equally have feared that a unilateral withdrawal in the face of Allied determination to leave their forces in Russia would poison chances for inter-Allied agreement on Russian and any other policy positions. In short, Wilson kept American troops in Russia because he felt that their removal would endanger his much broader world vision.[9]

Not everyone shared the Wilsonian commitment to joint action. In fact, the United States may have been the only major power to withhold action in Russia pending inter-Allied agreement. Certainly Japan did not, as its increase in troop number and economic activity indicated. Ironically, the Japanese increased their economic penetration in Siberia just when American efforts began gearing down following the armistice. After learning of the Russian Bureau's originally proposed scope of operation, the Japanese private sector had been critical of its government's inaction. In late December the government and financiers agreed to establish a Japanese Siberian Economic Commission "for relief work in Siberia." Whether the United States would respond to Japan's economic actions would depend on what it decided to do with the Russian Bureau now that the war was over. The State Department was upset enough about Japan's military and political activities to try to secure from the European Allies a joint expression of concern which it hoped would exert a restraining influence on the Asian Ally.[10]

Wilson was unwilling to pursue unilateral postarmistice programs in Siberia until a modus vivendi could be worked out with Japan, whose activities, many American observers thought, were undercutting any benefits from such programs. Not only did the Japanese military operations disrupt the normalization of conditions in Siberia but, because of America's association with Japan as an interventionist force, its actions damaged America's reputation among the local inhabitants. Negotiations to settle some of these difficulties were completed by January 1919. The resultant agreement dealt primarily with understandings as to the proper operation of the railroad network.[11]

While the impact of that agreement and of other forces operating on Wilson in Paris would affect the Russian Bureau, they did not resolve the broader Russian questions, upon which the United States was unable or unwilling to proceed without Allied concurrence. Since such agreements were few and far between, postarmistice policy proposals tended to die aborning or find themselves in suspended animation pending developments that never developed. As a result, the United States was left without a discernible, coherent postwar policy toward Russia of its own and without agreement on any such policies with the Allies.

As the primary source of the food needed by much of war-damaged Europe, the United States was, however, in a position to do something about Bolshevism, which was the direct antithesis of capitalism and therefore incompatible with America's and the world's economic well-being. Preserving these areas from Bolshevism would not only stop this threat but, in the process, open doors for American economic exploration which earlier had been monopolized by their respective empires—German, Austro-Hungarian, or Russian. That, at least, was the thrust of a memorandum Herbert Hoover, in charge of the European relief program, sent to the American Peace Commissioners in mid-February 1919.[12]

Food was a vital ingredient of America's international attack on Bolshevism. Well-fed, prosperous people do not fall prey to the corruptive appeal of communism, or so the argument ran. The food policy attacked Bolshevism as an ideological phenomenon. Its implementation was not restricted to Russia. Wherever applied, its proponents wanted to "preserve these countries from Bolshevism and rank anarchy." Americans recognized that military destruction of men would not alleviate the depressed conditions responsible for the ideology's potency.

General Tasker Bliss thought the chaos in Europe could only be solved by speeding peace, opening eastern Europe to commercial activity, feeding people, helping cultivate fields, and reestablishing industry and a sense of interdependence. The early planners of economic assistance to Russia had been thinking along similar lines even before the Bolsheviks had assumed significance as a power reality in Russia.[13]

While no such sweeping program to reconstruct war-torn Europe materialized in time to affect the peace conference, food relief did become a bribe used to keep areas from espousing the radical ideology. Herbert Hoover had no qualms about using food to achieve political goals. He did so in Romania (to keep it from waging war) and in Hungary (to overthrow the communist Bela Kun regime).[14]

Ironically, Russia itself had, in the past, been the food reserve of eastern Europe. Aware that Russian agricultural resources could "help feed eastern Europe and quell disruption there," American policy-makers found the emergence of a non-Bolshevik Russia that much more imperative to a Wilsonian world. Russia could help stop Bolshevism.[15] Thus, although Hoover's food relief had no direct contact with the Russian Bureau's programs, there was a logical correlation. If Russia could be "saved," it could contribute—as Wilson had always thought it might—to building a better, peaceful world.

There is, however, a not so subtle difference between the Russian Bureau's relief work and Hoover's food relief program. The first, as originally designed, would help the Rus-

sians help themselves—an optimistic policy based on the
perception of a revolutionary Russian population ready and
willing to espouse progressive ideas. This first idea carried
few if any overtones of charity. The second, a more defensive
and pessimistic approach, would force populations to reject
ideology in favor of food. One wanted to help Russia; the
other, to hurt Bolshevism. Both programs contributed to the
same overall Wilsonian foreign policy although the approaches differed and the peoples and regions involved often
seemed to have little in common.

Americans at Paris even tried to get the Bolsheviks to
agree to their own ideological destruction—assuming that
adequate food really would immunize people against communism—by proposing a massive food relief program for
persons inside Bolshevik territory. There were two "provisos" to the offer: a cease-fire in the ongoing civil war must
go into effect in all targeted areas and outside agents must
be responsible for the distribution of relief. Since the cease-
fire might not have been observed by the anti-Bolshevik
Russian forces, and since abdication of responsibility in relief distribution would have undercut their control over the
population, the Bolsheviks rejected these provisos. The
United States did not, therefore, succeed in feeding Bolshevism to death inside Russia.[16]

There remained, on the economic front, economic strangulation as a weapon for combating Bolshevism in Russia.
The wartime blockade of the Central Powers had been ex-
tended to cover Bolshevik Russia when it began its separate
peace negotiations. The general blockade remained more or
less in effect until Germany signed the Paris peace treaty in
June 1919. Since, according to Herbert Hoover, "the entire
American group at Paris, from the President down considered a rigid blockade [of Central Europe] utter folly because
it created unemployment, prevented economic recovery and
fertilized Communism," it was pleased, therefore, when this
general blockade ended. That blockade was replaced almost
immediately by one against Bolshevik Russia alone. This
singularly Russian blockade would remain in effect as offi-

cial peace conference—and unofficial American—policy until January 1920.[17]

Thus, by the spring and summer of 1919, the United States and the Allies had decided on a dual, if unofficial, policy toward Bolshevism: they would try an aggressive program of economic strangulation inside the Bolshevik lines and a preventative economic, or food, program outside the Red Army's reach. Hoover obviously had Wilson's approval to continue his food war in European Russia; but what role could or would the Russian Bureau play from its vantage points in northern and far eastern Russia? A continuation of the food relief programs in Europe after war's end did not face the same obstacles confronting the Russian Bureau. The bureau was, after all, primarily a facilitator of trade, not of charity, and it had depended on both private sector interest *and* government regulation to ensure desirable commercial relief efforts.

American business had begun to strain under wartime regulation. Demanding licensing and distributional controls, the War Trade Board in general and the Russian Bureau in particular personified governmental and bureaucratic constraints of free trade. Whether rightly or not, businessmen had come to associate the bureau with commercial restriction rather than commercial expansion. Never a popular phenomenon even under the pressing needs of a military emergency, regulation drew hostile criticism once the guns stopped. From a commercial perspective, many Americans saw the bureau's continued operation as both unnecessary and undesirable. If the United States government as distinct from the American business community wanted to embark on any sizable peacetime economic operation in Russia, using public money and demanding bureaucratic regulations, it would meet heavy resistance from the business community. That a coordinated, governmentally controlled relief effort would focus more pertinently on Russia's real needs than would random private sector trade arrangements does not seem to have carried much weight. In fairness, government planners themselves made little effort to argue the point.

Public antipathy, added to the anticipated dismantling of all war bureaucracies and to Wilson's predilection for inter-Allied, rather than unilateral, programs in postwar Russia, all raised obvious questions about the Russian Bureau's future. Some of the bureau's personnel shared the businessmen's aversion to peacetime government interference in the private sector's domain. Even those who did not understood the need to avoid the appearance of government interference. From the bureau's beginning, care had been taken to present its own $5 million fund as in no way intended to compete with private capital. At a staff meeting in early November 1918, the bureau's manager, H. B. Van Sinderin, stressed the importance of avoiding any impression that the United States government was itself entering "into any great program in Russia." The public was to be told that since "commercial conditions" in Russia were "somewhat different than those existing in other countries" it would "be necessary to depart from the procedure employed in other countries."[18] With the war over, the bureau would find it all the more difficult to justify continuation of regulations and controls, much less use of the revolving fund. Washington Russia-watchers had good reason to believe that neither the public nor Congress wanted to use tax money in peacetime to finance Wilson's vision of an economically induced "revolutionary Russia." Retrenchment in government finances and foreign involvements was clearly the order of the day.

If Wilson did arrive at acceptable inter-Allied policies, they would probably involve continued publicly financed economic expenditures at which Congress and the public might well balk. On the other hand, the Allies might also balk. A December in-house memorandum summarized the international nature of the bureau's dilemma: "The position of the United States in the economic rehabilitation of Russia should be determined at the Peace Conference. It is believed no projects can be effected in a broad sense without inter-Allied cooperation, which up to the present it has been impossible to obtain." Russian Bureau personnel had good reason to fear for their program's future in spite of Wilson's avowed determination to help the Russians.[19]

The armistice had had no measurable impact on Russian Bureau operations until well into December. But thereafter, the Washington office projected a noticeable drop in enthusiasm. Heid was told not to assume any additional "liability" but, within that limitation, to continue transmitting "prospective orders from buyers in Russia." He was also to keep sending information on Russia's available exports and commodity needs, "which information will be made known to interested merchants here who we believe will shortly be in a position to carry on the trade." The bureau halted in midstream—"in view of uncertain status of Bureau"—plans to act as middleman between the War Department and purchasers in Russia. However, the bureau did ask the War Department to consider taking over such sales itself and told Heid that, if it agreed to do so, he was to provide as much assistance as possible short of incurring financial obligations. Heid was also informed that the bureau's merchandising of samples had been abandoned and that he should sell what goods he had on hand as soon as possible.[20]

In preparation for the peace conference and for their own possible job termination, bureau personnel set about analyzing their agency's past rationales, present circumstances, and future potential. When the trade controls were lifted, as they were sure to be and in some cases already had been, trade could no longer be regulated so as "to insure Russian consumers receiving American merchandise at fair prices." This had been a primary bureau objective. A second original purpose had been to supply Russia with goods not "served readily by private enterprise." The bureau staff thought it now even less likely, in the face of increasing environmental uncertainties, that private capital would be interested in risky undertakings in Russia. Thus the volume of goods needed in Russia but not "served readily by private enterprise" would probably actually increase as trade opportunities elsewhere attracted merchants away from Russia. While this suggested a parallel increase in bureau use of its own funds to satisfy Russia's needs, the staff recognized, perhaps belatedly, that $5 million could "do very little to render the amount of economic aid which is required" even if it had been inclined to try. Facing a seemingly insoluble situation, the staff reasoned that many of the services for which the bureau had originally been established were either no longer needed or impossible to perform. The most logical solution would be to eliminate the bureau or, at the very least, redefine its purpose.[21]

On December 26, 1918, the Washington Russian Bureau office informed the American peace delegation to Paris that the status of the bureau was "anomalous" because "the company has become, or will soon become, a competitor of American and foreign private capital without at the same time being able to effect a proper control of Russian trade which was one of the primary reasons for its existence." If the bureau continued its originally intended operations it would be resented "by the public and by the commercial interests and governments of friendly countries."[22]

On the other hand, there were still a few functions that the bureau could "properly perform." It could provide transitional transportation and financial services until shipping lines and banks could get established in Russia, work to increase the shipping tonnage available for trade in articles most urgently needed in Russia, and continue investigating for and providing information about projects of interest to private capital. And finally, the bureau might serve as a go-between in negotiating the sale, in Russia, of United States government war surplus materials which the government, for political reasons, was unwilling to factor out to private capital.[23]

Vance McCormick told the Paris delegation that the bureau would "carry on," but that he had ordered it to incur no obligations which could not be fully discharged upon dissolution of the War Trade Board or which could not be picked up by some other government agency. He felt that no one country could significantly influence the economic direction of postwar Russia:

> If it is desirable to continue the supervision and direction of Russian foreign trade, this can be effected only through the adoption of some comprehensive scheme

for a control by the associated governments of all merchandise entering or coming from Russia and Siberia; and it further appears that any such scheme must involve the establishment of an interallied control upon Russian ground and the establishment of control organizations at all the gateways of Russia.

Action would have to wait on agreements arrived at in Paris, but McCormick did suggest that the Russian Bureau might have a future life as the nucleus of such an inter-Allied program.[24]

On January 3, 1919, the War Trade Board notified American merchants that commodities not still on the restricted lists could be shipped directly to buyers in Russia and no longer had to be consigned to Heid. Thus the field office lost control over American-Russian commerce. By mid-January, with only a few exceptions, licenses were being issued freely "for all commodities produced in and shipped from Russia," thereby reflecting a marked relaxation of the Board's restrictions on, and supervision of, commerce at the American end.[25]

Also by mid-January McCormick, who it will be remembered was chairman of the War Trade Board as well as bureau president, joined Wilson in Paris as a special adviser. Keeping the peace delegation informed of developments at home, the bureau's Washington manager reported that the office staff had been "very much cut down" in size but that he was awaiting word from Paris before taking any reductive measures at the Vladivostok end. Also relayed to Paris was the text of a press release informing the public that the "entire situation" had been "changed by the signing of the Armistice." The bureau would remain open, the release reassured its readers, in an advisory capacity only, for whosoever might be able to use its services—public or private. The bureau would not, the release stressed, be competing with private commercial interests.[26]

This release must have been an attempt to undercut the postarmistice resentment of continued government controls.

The bureau's vice-president, Clarence Woolley, had already told McCormick that the "psychology of the country is adverse to any form of Government control of business, which tendency increases as the increasing business depression becomes more accentuated, together with constantly increasing unemployment." As one of the few still operating controls—i.e., licensing of trade with Russia—the bureau had become the butt of much criticism.[27]

The Washington office initiated all of these moves to curtail bureau activity. Wilson had sent no orders to that effect and the moves were made with little consideration for how such activity might be interpreted in Russia. The bureau was reacting to public pressure at home and to the foreseeable demise of wartime control agencies such as itself.

Americans in the field, on the other hand, saw a need for continuation and perhaps even expansion of the Russian Bureau. Ambassador Paul Reinsch, cabling from China, told the State Department that

> There is strong feeling among many Russians that the American Government [is not willing] to help Russians unless guaranteed concession and commercial advantages. This feeling increased by efforts of our Consular and commercial offices to collect information regarding economic and commercial assets and needs of Siberia. The Russians want help in establishing sound government and look to America as democratic government for assistance. Our declared desire to help Russian people has hollow ring, when they need everything and can obtain nothing from us.

Only by engaging in government-sponsored, nonexploitative economic assistance could the United States protect its image as a true friend of the Russian people.[28]

Reinsch's argument was seconded by the continuing inflow of suggestions on how America could help Russia that had been arriving at various government offices ever since the March Russian revolution. Most of these proposals assumed a future Russia freed from the Bolshevik regime. One academician reminded the State Department that Germany was still in the best position to control Russia economically. He wanted America and the Allies actively to involve themselves in Russian financial institutions to ensure that they, and not Germany, would benefit from the inevitable reconstruction and reorganization of Russia's economy. He also wanted to see continued trade and even recommended that the government provide risk insurance to businesses engaged in intercourse with Russia. At least two Russians argued that the existence (or nonexistence) of economic assistance would determine Russia's future attitude toward America and the Allies. They warned that if assistance did not come from those quarters Russia would be forced to turn to Germany. Neither of these American and Russian pleas for continued economic assistance differentiated between various political factions currently fighting inside Russia; nor did they make specific recommendations as to the domestic utilization of such "assistance" inside Russia.[29]

Another group of Russians in America offered more "political" suggestions, calling for help in establishing "legal, educational and commercial institutions [in Russia] based on methods employed in America." In the distribution of food and supplies and procurement of needed agricultural machinery, supplies and education, this group advocated coordinated commercial and industrial assistance, with government control over private transactions (not exactly one of America's own commercial methods). It also suggested that "where possible an exchange of manufactured foods and purchases of game, fish and other foods which might be found in abundance be encouraged in order to bring about a gradual rebuilding of the industrial market" and, presumably, ease the exchange problems a currency transaction would entail. Such a proposal was "wide-spectrum" and would have incorporated economic assistance into a broad reform effort in Russia.[30]

The authors of these various plans were either unaware of the Russian Bureau's existence, assumed that it was a wartime agency soon to be abolished, or thought in much grander financial terms than the bureau's capitalization could accommodate. They also appeared oblivious to the suspicion with which many Americans viewed government peacetime involvement directly in the economy of this or any other country. Indeed, they all seemed to be arguing that American policy toward Russia must transcend such traditional reluctances toward foreign involvements. In summary, outside the Russian Bureau loud voices urged a continuation of the government's economic relief efforts.

By late January the Paris delegation had had time to assimilate the various suggestions, public and private, from both the United States and Russia. Policy-makers in Paris gave a broader reading to events than did the bureau staff at home. They also may have been less attuned to the economic "atmosphere" at home. McCormick cabled the Washington office that it would be very unfortunate if Siberia got the impression that the bureau was closing down. Instead, he wanted to create the idea that recent "relative inactivity" resulted not from an abandonment of the Russian people but from the belief that assistance could now best be rendered through "regular channels of trade," with government intercession no longer necessary.[31]

On February 3, 1919, Woodrow Wilson himself breathed new life into the bureau. He indicated that continued aid to Russia was even more important now than it had been before the armistice and that the bureau still had a commercial and financial role to play. Wilson wanted it to "proceed irrespective of possible Congressional criticism" and left to its discretion the "extent to which Congress shall be kept advised of activities." The President suggested that the bureau might even want to broaden its areas of operation to include southern Russia, which he understood was now one of the more promising centers of commercial activity still free of Bolshevism and therefore open to programs aimed at helping the Russians help themselves.[32]

This revitalization message suggests several things about Wilson's thinking. One, Wilson still felt strongly committed to helping the Russians help themselves—strongly enough, in fact, to ignore Congressional opposition and to continue a program for which there was no peacetime precedent. Second, he seems to have adopted a rather firm anti-Bolshevik stance. The bureau might broaden its operation but it was still limited to areas free of radical control, even though there was now absolutely no war-related justification for the distinction. And finally, the message suggests a presidential unawareness of the obstacles confronting Russian Bureau efforts.

While both McCormick and Wilson said the bureau should actively carry on its work, neither clarified just what that work would now be. Could the bureau use its capital fund to enter the trade market itself should private capital not be forthcoming? Would more money be available if needed? Would the transportation and currency situations be improved? Or was the bureau's postarmistice work now to be limited to facilitation?

The February 3 message gave no answers to these questions. Wilson never suggested redefining or reorganizing the bureau. He did nothing to stop the lifting of trade restrictions to and from Russia. Even though the Russian, American, and international environments in which the bureau operated had all altered dramatically, the bureau's charter remained unchanged.[33]

Nevertheless, the postarmistice hiatus had ended. Within its range of feasible operations, the Russian Bureau was still on the job. But the Washington office continued to reiterate that it could do little that would not compete with private capital. And any major economic program would presumably need to be multinational. Wilson's postarmistice charge to the bureau suggests, therefore, that he was more concerned with telling revolutionary Russia that the Government of the United States was committed to its well-being and that American interests were not simply limited to the profit and loss columns of private enterprise than he was with the actual dollars and cents amount of trade resulting from bureau activity.[34]

FIVE

The Bureau in 1919

However well-meaning Wilson's words of revitalization, the Russian Bureau faced, in early 1919, even greater obstacles than it had faced in late 1918. The war was over although a peace had not yet been signed. Consequently, the war-emergency atmosphere which had provided at least part of the impetus to a government economic effort in Russia was also gone. The Russian Bureau's parent agency, the War Trade Board, was supposed to terminate operations as soon after the war as possible. In Russia, the civil war raged and solutions to that country's currency and transportation difficulties were no nearer at hand. In America, private capital looked for the most lucrative investments and resented government regulation of, and involvement in, foreign trade. And, with the reopening of European markets, Russian trade, with all its difficulties, attracted less interest than it had during the war.

In spite of these realities, anyone reading A. A. Boublikoff's February 1919 analysis of postwar international economics might well have been convinced that America had a vital stake in increasing its level of trade with Russia. Boublikoff, a former member of the Russian Duma, published a report linking Russia's economic recovery, under a non-Bolshevik government of course, directly to America's own economic well-being.[1]

Boublikoff began his argument by noting that the economic collapse of Russia had deprived the world of 180 million consumers of its surplus production. Since a redress of the trade balance would be the most important single solution to postwar economic dislocation, this was no mean statistic. The problem, of course, would be in financing Russia's purchasing ability. Technically, the redress of an international trade imbalance is, by definition, international in scope. But Boublikoff used America's emergence from the war as such an overwhelming creditor nation and the unlikelihood that other nations would want to increase their indebtedness to the United States to conclude that Russia would probably be the only major market open to American surplus goods. Without some outlet for the surplus, Boublikoff ominously warned that the domestic repercussions in America would be staggering. He predicted, therefore, that "the *economic destinies of Russia and American are bound together by indissoluble ties.*"[2]

Financing represented the single barrier to the successful resolution of America's surplus and Russia's need. And according to Boublikoff there were two "fundamental difficulties": "the absence in Russia of a regime of law and order" and "the collapse of the Russian monetary system." It followed, he reasoned, that the overthrow of the Bolsheviks became an American problem "upon purely business considerations" since commerce could not go forward under the existing conditions. The currency problem could be solved, he believed, by the creation of a private banking institution, uncorrupted by whatever domestic Russian political climate prevailed, which could issue exchange of an international (and therefore confident) character unhindered by the problems of printing press fever or inflation and controlled in such a way as to guarantee recirculation rather than hoarding. Boublikoff concluded his treatise with the prediction that only after the political and currency problems had been solved could it be possible "to expect that Russia can be supplied with the necessary goods and capital, and America secure for herself a broad consumers' market and thereby avert the enforced curtailment of her industry and all the social and political consequences of this."[3]

Boublikoff's rather nonspecific plans for future American-Russian interdependence made intriguing reading but failed to deal on a practical level with the *current* situation. The ongoing civil war made it clear that the Bolsheviks had not been overthrown; his projections assumed that such would be the case before recovery could begin. He did not anticipate that other countries might also be in need of markets and would be competing with the United States for Russia's consumers. Americans were particularly concerned about Japan and England as competitors. Nor did Boublikoff have any suggestions to offer about tackling the immediate currency and transportation problems still obstructing Russian Bureau efforts to promote American-Russian trade. And finally, Boublikoff could not anticipate that, while the United States government eagerly encouraged private sector trade, it would often shy away from its own financing of economic relief measures—not to mention its reluctance to participate actively in the overthrow of the Bolsheviks. Unwillingness to spend even the money already allocated to the Russian Bureau plagued that agency's final months.

During 1919 the Russian Bureau continued to promote and facilitate private sector trade by dispersing information, processing and "expediting" export and import licenses for both Siberia and northern Russia, and shipping commodity samples already in the pipeline. It continued to function as an interagency clearinghouse. For example, it screened all export licenses for "any material of political significance, this at request of State Department," and it handled "details of special committee of the President in the matter of Cze-cho-Slovak supplies." Some of the work, such as collecting freight charges owed on goods already shipped on vessels operated by the bureau and adjusting the affected Russian Bureau and other government accounts, was primarily book-keeping. And some of it falls into a catchall category: trying to establish a "banking connection" in the United States for the State Bank of Archangel (but encountering some diffi-culty) and helping the Russian Embassy get vessels from the Shipping Board to transport railroad materials to Vladivos-tok.[4]

But the bureau did not undertake new commercial or supply transactions on its own account. The Washington office insisted that it "could not now accomplish in Siberia any more useful purpose than a private trader." In spite of Wilson's statement that the bureau's work was even more important now than it had been in the past, Heid was ad-vised that the bureau "is not prepared to proceed with its program as originally conceived." In other words, it was no longer prepared to "engage actively in the supply to Siberia and North Russia of such commodities as would not, because of the inherent risk involved or for some other reason, be supplied by private interests." Even if he now wanted to—and in at least one case he did[5]—Heid no longer had access to the bureau's capital fund. The home office reasoned that "private merchants are now prepared to ship all commodi-ties for which tonnage can be procured, and which the dock-ing and warehouse facilities at Vladivostok are prepared to accommodate."[6]

Wilson's rhetorical revitalization to the contrary notwith-standing, the home office started restricting field options. That retrenchment was in part a response to conditions, in part a response to personal concepts of the proper role a government should play in international commerce. Unfor-tunately, the records do not indicate how the bureau's staff or directors reacted to Wilson's message from Paris or whether they *consciously* tried to restrict, rather than ex-pand, operations. There is also no evidence of Wilson's re-sponse, if any, to the bureau's actions.

On April 1, 1919, William Stanert, who had replaced Van Sinderin as bureau manager in December 1918, submitted a report which implied that the limitations on bureau operations were not of its own choosing. He noted "practically no change" in the status of bureau work in Siberia. The main difficulty remained lack of tonnage, "railroad material very badly needed for the upbuilding of the Trans-Siberian Railroad not having been transported" for that reason. As a consequence, Stanert recommended that the bureau do everything it could to upgrade both shipping and rail transportation. The implication was that a solution to the transportation problem would lead to a spurt in commercial intercourse. In Archangel, "rationing" continued and a proposal to supply seed to the area had been approved by the inter-Allied committee supervising the Murmansk Fund. Stanert mentioned bureau interest and business activity in the Black Sea areas. He indicated that much licensing had been granted but, since there was no tonnage available, little actual trade had taken place. Negotiations to sell war surplus goods to Siberian cooperative societies were underway and he hoped similar arrangements might be made with southern cooperatives. The bureau continued to try to "enlist the aid of the various American manufacturers in a specific plan to render economic aid to Russia and Siberia." Whatever the fate of the bureau itself, Stanert wrote, he hoped that American economic involvement in Russia would go forward.[7]

This report suggests that, while the bureau was willing to continue its role as trade facilitator, it was not willing to be an active trade participant. This may have been because of bureau hesitancy; it may also have been the natural response to news that all unexpended portions of wartime appropriations—one of which was the bureau capitalization—were to be returned to the Treasury as soon as possible. The evidence for trying to decide who was more responsible for limiting bureau operations—the bureau or the president—is ambiguous. In some instances the president seems to have urged expansion and encountered bureau resistance. But in other cases, as we shall see, the president was even less willing to spend government money in direct trade related expenditures than was the bureau.

The Russian Bureau's Washington office thought that there was "every desire on the part of private interests, both Russian and American, to engage in the shipment of commodities to and from Siberia, but this commerce is strictly limited for the present by a serious lack of facilities for transportation and distribution." Did this mean government-funded supply shipments could or should try to satisfy Russian demand? The bureau said no. Any dealings it undertook would face exactly the same difficulties and would take "a like amount of business . . . away from private commercial houses."[8] From this line of reasoning, it seems clear that the home office saw no reason to tap its capital fund to supply relief to Russia available from the private sector. But would it be willing to use its funds to finance relief efforts that were not in direct competition with the private sector? This question arose in regard to the possible sale, to Russian cooperative societies, of War Department surplus. And since this transaction sheds some light on what kind of relief financing the bureau and/or the president would agree to, it seems appropriate here, even though it is a little out of chronological order.

One of the Russian Bureau's most successful undertakings involved the Russian cooperative societies and the United States War Department. In spite of some in-house opposition, most of the bureau staff thought their agency might play a constructive role in negotiations with the seemingly stable cooperative organizations. Millions of individual farmers and communes and agricultural businesses belonged to such societies. Representing their collective membership, the cooperatives could buy, sell, distribute, and finance both imports and exports with much greater efficiency than could be achieved among the general population in any other way. Throughout 1918 various people had suggested that the cooperatives would be good economic contacts in establishing Russian-American trade relations. There were believed to be sound political inducements as

well. According to H. L. Huntington, the person responsible
for Russian affairs at the Bureau of Foreign and Domestic
Commerce, Russian cooperatives were "exceedingly democratic and nonpolitical," with the politics of the average
member being "moderate socialism." Huntington thought
the cooperatives would come to "occupy a greater and
greater place in Russian life, as [they are] a training school
of constructive democracy, and one of the chief sources
whence we may expect the future sound and self-respecting
middle class of Russia, the class which she has so lacked up
to the present time." He also reasoned that although the
cooperatives were generally anti-Bolshevik, they had es-
caped the radical wrath because they were "too near the
hearts and pocketbooks of the plain people" for anyone to
risk challenging them. As a result, the cooperative movement throughout the country was the only business and
financial "apparatus still functioning in the chaos of Bolshevik Russia." Cooperatives fortunate enough to be located
outside Bolshevik territory were simply that much more
stable.[9]

In early March 1919, the Union of Siberian Creamery
Associations and the Union of the Siberian Cooperative Associations made inquiries in Washington about a several
million dollar loan, possibly from the Russian Bureau itself,
which they would use to buy American goods for distribution
in Siberia and repay with the sales proceeds. The cooperatives agreed that the entire operation, from purchasing
through distribution, would be supervised by American
agents in the field. The same unions also proposed that they
buy surplus supplies from the War Department on an additional credit. These were the supplies which the bureau itself
had been planning to purchase for resale in Russia when the
armistice halted negotiations. If this second idea materialized, the bureau would act as a "clearing house." The credit
would be established directly with the War Department, and
the bureau would, in this instance, assume no financial liability but merely supervise distribution. The bureau management in Washington told Heid that "we realize [the]

difficulty in attempting control of this kind and [the] impossibility of controlling price after first sale, but our main idea is to secure distribution of needed articles and believe that if enough are sent into Siberia prices will be regulated automatically."[10]

The "distribution of needed articles" was not quite all the United States hoped such dealings might accomplish. As the bureau told Ambassador Morris,

> The thought is already entertained that if this government manifests an interest in these cooperatives as representing a large body of non-Bolshevik Russian population, and offers the substantial encouragement expressed by the extension of credit . . . , the political effect thereof will be advantageous while the benefits to American trade likewise will be important in establishing close and permanent connections between this country and the cooperatives.

There is a strong suggestion of State Department wording in this message and it also contains one of the most overt pronouncements of America's desire to encourage Russia's political future—obviously along anti-Bolshevik lines. On the other hand, cooperatives were not seen as comparable to political or military "factions" and American policy-makers may have reasoned that since they represented the Russian people as opposed to Russian politicians, dealings with them did not constitute "interference" in Russia's internal affairs. As we shall see, August Heid did not exclude cooperative society officials from the ranks of "politician" even though he did agree that the organizations would provide good points of distribution for commodities needed in Russia.[11]

The bureau asked American officials in Siberia for their opinions. Was there any adverse political significance in making loans to these groups? Were these two cooperatives the proper groups to work through? What other groups might be included? How could the transactions be supervised?[12]

Heid had earlier made reference to political implications in dealing with anybody in Russia:

In our opinion the choice of organization or agency of distribution all should pend a more definite crystallization of the political situation. . . . Many Russian politicians are not so much concerned about economic relief as about the use of relief to obtain preferment for themselves. Opportunity of employing economic relief to obtain political advantage is afforded the officials of the Creamery Association [in this particular instance] by committing to them such large quantities of machinery and other commodities.

He wanted to avoid letting officials take advantage of their opportunities by insisting that some American representative be the person actually to turn the machinery or commodities over to their designated recipients. His concerns about controlling the distribution of War Department surpluses reflected the same desire to avoid giving anyone the chance to "obtain political advantage."[13]

Ambassador Morris, replying to the bureau's query, indicated that everyone he had talked to agreed on the advisability of extending credits to the cooperatives provided it could be done in such a manner as to allow Heid control over distribution and pricing. The Bureau of Foreign and Domestic Commerce felt no need to add such provisos when explaining the proposed transactions domestically and simply told inquirers that the United States supported Russian cooperatives because they were "democratic organizations."[14]

By April 22 Heid had sent in his full report and recommendations on the proposed dealings with cooperative societies. In general, he supported both the sales and loans, believing that they might "fully and satisfactorily take the place of the program of the Russian Bureau, Incorporated, as originally formulated." He did want to make sure tight controls could be exercised over procedures and distribution. He also reported that the financial status of the societies was weak owing to the problems with rail transportation, the depreciated currency, and the lack of export traffic. Nevertheless, he did not think the credit risk hazardous since the cooperatives would ultimately be able to supply raw materials in exchange for the goods. Ordinary direct sales were "now out of the question" because of the currency problems, so a barter procedure would be ideal. Now, in the spring of 1919, Heid felt that the need for economic aid to Siberia was "urgent," and would have the twofold advantage of directing the affected Russian population—most of whom were as a class non-Bolshevik—"into more normal and rational ways of life" and counteracting "the present anti-American propensity which otherwise may jeopardize Russian American commercial relations for years to come and discount efforts and monetary expenditures to date of military[,] Red Cross and YMCA." Heid argued that this "opportunity [of] commencing trade relations . . . should not be overlooked," especially since Great Britain and Japan had already "shipped large quantit[ies] of goods and will almost exclude American products unless prompt action is taken."[15]

His recommendation to omit the Union of Siberian Cooperative Associations from any dealings and to substitute the Union of Siberian Credit Unions, Zemstvo Union, and Immigration Bureau met with no problems either in America or Russia and was implemented in later negotiations. As for the War Department materials, Heid favored distribution by the War Department itself, "thus creating good will amongst Russians toward American Expeditionary Force," but when the department rejected that suggestion he seems to have readily accepted the bureau's role.[16]

Consul General Caldwell, in Vladivostok, agreed with Heid that "preference be given Siberian cooperative credit societies and creamery associations," at least until the currency situation improved—presumably because they were in the best position to exchange goods for goods. He hoped that if things went according to plan the railroads would soon be able to handle volume shipments such as the sales to cooperatives would entail.[17] Caldwell's comments make it clear that currency and transportation remained the biggest obstacles to "normal" economic relations in Russia.

Having gotten the support of Americans in Siberia for both the loan and the War Department sales, the bureau now discovered an obstacle to the loan. In early 1919 President Wilson had requested that the Treasury Department secure the return of all funds allotted during the war for "National Security and Defense," one appropriation of which had been the bureau's capital fund. This line item designation covered a wide variety of wartime appropriations. Administratively, with peace seemingly at hand, it made sense to begin closing down wartime agencies. There is no reason to believe that Wilson, in this decision, was singling out the Russian Bureau for expiration or even, for that matter, that he knew the bureau would be affected. After all, at about the same time he had told it to expand its operations. Nevertheless, the return of "National Security and Defense" funds would have killed the bureau. The directors asked McCormick, still in Paris, to "confer with the President and ascertain whether the demands of the Treasury are more important than the benefits to Russia which would result from" loaning the money to the cooperatives. In this instance, the recall of war appropriations, and not the bureau's own reluctance, threatened to hamstring American relief efforts for Russia unless an exception could be made.[18]

On April 2 McCormick approved establishing contracts with the cooperatives, but rejected a direct bureau-to-cooperative loan. There was some question as to the propriety of the bureau engaging in such activity—the government did not normally loan money to private organizations either at home or abroad—and there was also the possibility that the bureau might terminate before the transactions had been completed. (The projected loan payback periods had ranged up to two years.) As would become apparent in another context, the presidential recall of "National Defense" funds would not have stood in the way had there been no other objections. It is difficult to decide whether Wilson's unwillingness to loan bureau funds did in fact hinge on the time factor or was simply another sign of his hesitation to spend "real money" as part of a government-financed assistance program. The bureau, in this case, seemed more than willing to loan as much as $3.5 million to the cooperatives.[19]

McCormick, with the president's concurrence, did suggest that the War Department, via the Board of Liquidation, carry out dealings directly with the cooperatives and, at the same time, name the bureau as one of the department's liquidation agencies so that it could, while it remained active, handle the War Department part of the cooperatives' proposal. In this more traditional situation of sale of surplus goods, there was little hesitation on Wilson's part.[20]

The bureau quickly conferred with the War Department and told Heid about the arrangements worked out:

> War department here willing to cooperate with bureau ... but unwilling to undertake this matter alone. Russian Bureau would not purchase War Department supplies but would act in supervisory capacity only. Creamery Associations would be required to sign a carefully prepared agreement which would cover all the suggestions mentioned [in] your various cables on this subject [re distribution and controls], and Russian Bureau here and abroad would organize for supervisory purposes only.

In short, the bureau would be acting as agent rather than actual participant in these sales.[21]

After several months of negotiations, the terms of bureau involvement in dealings with the cooperatives were arranged. There would be no direct loan from the capital fund to the societies. But the board of directors authorized the bureau, if requested, to act as an "agency of the Army Liquidation Board," without expense to the War Department, in the proposed sales by that board to Russian cooperative societies. There were two provisos: that the bureau might "retire from such activities at any time," and that the bureau should incur no nonadministrative financial obligations.[22]

In late June the bureau staff learned that the War Department had in fact signed contracts with the cooperatives (for what goods and upon what terms are not now clear) and was "willing to sign additional contracts with other societies." The action was "prompted not by business consideration but on [the] desire to carry out this Government['s] purpose to assist [the] Russian people."[23]

Wilson was still committed to helping the Russian people, and he was willing to risk government (i.e., War Department) goods and money to do so. But he was not willing to let the agency specifically created for that purpose risk *its* capital fund to the same end, even though the bureau agreed to do so. Had Wilson never seriously expected the Russian Bureau to use its capital fund? Since, at approximately the same time he disapproved bureau loans to the cooperatives, he had suggested expansion of the bureau's scope of operation, it would appear that he viewed it primarily as a relief facilitator—not as an active relief financer. This would, at least, seem to be how the War Trade Board interpreted Wilson's intentions, although anticipation of the bureau's and its own termination may have had as much to do with the board's decision to keep the bureau limited in scope to northern and eastern Russia.

Wilson, it will be remembered, had suggested that the bureau might want to expand its operations into south Russia, where reportedly needs were acute and exports available. During the war southern Russia had been outside the American areas of intervention and responsibility. Just as England and France had, theoretically, left Siberia to America and Japan, the United States had left the south to France and England. At war's end, southern Russia, like all of non-Bolshevik Russia, became less sensitive to earlier, interventionist division of responsibilities. Russians at Paris said the area needed clothing and a variety of heavy machinery; it had oil, tobacco, grain, and coal available to export.[24]

After some discussion, the War Trade Board decided that south Russia should be opened to general trade, rather than that specifically filtered through the Russian Bureau. In making that decision, the War Trade Board implicitly narrowed the bureau's scope of operation and thus can be seen as weaning it, and the government, away from economic commitments. The board was "prepared as far as possible to encourage private enterprises" to explore opportunities in the south, but such exploration would not be part of a coordinated relief program such as the bureau had originally conceived. As a result, the Russian Bureau had little contact with developments in south Russia. Since, in response to deteriorating conditions in Siberia, more private American attention did come to be focused on the south, a gap emerged between bureau emphasis and private interests. This gap seems, in hindsight, to parallel a flaw in bureau perceptions. If private capital was not attracted to Siberia—and that seems clearly the case—why not use bureau funds to import some of the small hardware items so much in demand? The circular answer seems to have been that private traders *could* do it, whether or not they actually *did* do it. The bureau may have rejected such direct involvement because of the theoretical competition with the private sector or because it assumed the president would disapprove.[25]

Whether or not the Russian Bureau could or would use its own funds, its primary goal of promoting private sector trade with Russia remained unchanged. And the private sector continued to express interest in such opportunities. Commerce Department files verify that throughout at least the first half of 1919 it was handling a great many requests for information on Russia. The Bureau of Foreign and Domestic Commerce even established an office of "modest proportions" to deal specifically with Russia. Commerce compiled a bibliography to which it referred inquiries, which included the State Department Foreign Trade Advisor's Office's "An Economic Study of Russia before and during the War," and Joseph Goldstein's "America's Opportunities for Trade and Investment in Russia," published by the Russian Information Bureau in New York. Russian Bureau manager William Stanert credited the bureau with opening the "ports of Russia on the Black Sea" to general trade by circulating information and facilitating licensing. He did note that not many Americans had taken advantage of this yet, even though the opportunities seemed numerous.[26]

In mid-March a long composite cable from various consuls in Asiatic Russia summarized economic opportunities open to interested American entrepreneurs. Among others, the report mentioned Russia's need for mining equipment and grain elevators—rather substantial capital investments. While one of the contributors argued against involvement by government (as opposed to private parties), another believed that the reported "curtailment" of the Russian Bureau's work was "coming at an inopportune time." Opportunities to promote private trade abounded. Since the bureau's "programme was too widely advertised in the beginning," its performance to date, not to mention any future cutback of activities, would be interpreted by the Russians as less than full compliance with America's commitment to provide reconstructive assistance.[27]

While it is clear that expressions of American business interest far outnumbered actual business transactions, one reason for the shortfall between promotional effort and actual trade may have originated at the Russian end. In April Heid complained that only about four of the American merchants currently doing business in Siberia projected a positive image of the integrity of American business. The remainder were "of a class whose operations" did little to help the "commercial reputation of the United States." Earlier, the consul general in Vladivostok had forwarded to the State Department a very derogatory article about American business practices written by a Russian recently returned from the United States. The Russian implied that great care had to be taken in trading with the United States in order to ensure receipt of quality merchandise, at fair prices, and delivered undamaged. The consul did not suggest that any kind of rebuttal would be in order, nor does the government seem to have taken any action to improve the caliber of American business representatives in Russia. This Russian indictment of American trade practices conflicts with other

Russian reports of a preference in dealing with Americans over the Allies. The discrepancy may have been simply idiosyncratic or it may have been a difference between someone who actually had dealt with Americans and others who would like to do so.[28]

If some Russians were worried about American business practices, more Americans were worried about Japanese business practices and Japanese intentions in Siberia. In late 1918 the American Russian Chamber of Commerce had warned the Commerce Department that Japan was "undertaking a very active campaign for the purpose of developing a close commercial rapprochement between Russian and Japanese interests and they have been able to make considerable headway." In February 1919, Secretary of Commerce Redfield heard rumors of Japan's purchase of American goods for resale in Russia at prices lower than those charged by American firms selling directly to Russia. Japan was accused of hiring Americans to duplicate American goods and services in order to undersell the United States in Siberia. The object, apparently, was to "undermine America commercially in Siberia, to kill our trade there, and to advance trade with Japan." These reports help explain why the government was so eager to encourage American trade with Russia and also so anxious to restrain Japanese activities there. They do not explain why the Japanese were willing to deal with Russia when American businesses apparently were not. Physical proximity suggests one reason for Japan's interest and for its apparent ability to undersell America.[29]

Geography alone does not explain the enthusiasm Great Britain—the other bête noire in Wilson's concern about exploitative economic penetration—showed for Russian trade links. During 1919 the Siberian Supply Company—organized and regulated by the British government and operating on a nonprofit basis to bring needed consumer goods to the area—delivered almost £300,000 worth of products to Siberia. While the expressed purpose for establishing this virtual twin of the Russian Bureau was "relief," England also had political and economic "nationalistic" motives. Politically, it wanted to encourage an independent Siberia. The Omsk-Kolchak government had close British ties and, in any case, such a subdivision of the old tsarist empire would present less of a threat to the British empire. Economically, the British government feared postwar Japanese and American monopolization of Russian markets and resources. It did not think England could successfully compete one-on-one against either America's or Japan's superior financial resources. The government attempted to retain an English share in Russia's "open door" by actively encouraging British business ventures and by championing joint, or inter-Allied programs in which it could obtain a guaranteed participation.[30] Ironically, both the English and the American governments were suspicious of each other—out of fear of their own economic inferiority. Both also had great difficulty attracting their respective private sectors to the cause.

During 1919 American advocates of an "open door" in Russia had more to worry about than the real or imagined English and Japanese competition. Two of the problems hampering American-Russian intercourse remained unresolved: currency and transportation.

American currency reform plans had come to a standstill at the war's end—pending an inter-Allied agreement at the peace conference. By early March 1919 the "certificate" plan outlined in December had been abandoned. In Paris, General Tasker Bliss perceptively predicted the unlikelihood of any joint Russian policy being arrived at, at least until the peace terms with Germany had been agreed upon and the Allies had stopped bickering with each other. As a result, on April 25 the United States government advised its diplomats in Archangel that the "currency situation must be dealt with on a hand to mouth basis for the present."[31]

Merchants encountered so many problems with the existing ruble that, in spite of special arrangements, little commercial activity developed. From Archangel, Felix Cole warned that "all sales be consummated in American or other stable non-Russian currency," and in no case should they "be made against rouble payment . . . because the absence of merchandise suitable for purchase and shipment to America ... as well as the shortage of foreign exchange holdings here render it impossible for the American seller to recover his funds." Cole saw the problem not so much as ruble depreciation but as ruble uselessness. From Siberia, Heid cabled that "Present ruling exchange at twenty roubles for one dollar [versus prewar rates of two for one] is prohibitive and private merchants cannot undertake risk of shipping commodities to Vladivostok." There would have been outlets for merchants to spend any rubles earned through trade, but the inflation rate undercut the possibility of making even a reasonable profit. Neither Cole nor Heid saw much prospect of private sector dealings in Russia so long as the ruble remained the only medium of exchange. In its economic dealings with the Russian cooperative societies, the United States government tried to solve the currency problem by establishing—as the Russian Bureau's financial expert had earlier suggested—credit and barter relations that bypassed the need for currency. The absence of War Department records of these sales makes it impossible to ascertain whether this arrangement was successful or whether, for that matter, the War Department ever got paid in whatever kind for its surplus goods.[32]

Transportation problems—both land and sea—also still persisted. But where currency difficulties limited the Russian Bureau's success as a trade facilitator, the plight of Russia's railroads—and their need for financing—quite literally helped bring the bureau to an end.

By March 1919 the war restrictions on shipping had been lifted, but with confusion reigning in Vladivostok's port facilities and with return cargoes in short supply, the shipping space shortage did not measurably improve. Given these and other difficulties associated with doing business in Russia, many businessmen were more eager to exploit the commercial opportunities once again available in recuperating Europe. Ships which during the war had been regulated out of the Russian trade lanes now voluntarily stayed clear. In April the Russian Bureau informed Heid that it was having "trouble getting railroad supplies" to him for delivery to

Stevens "because reports of the terrible congestion in Vladivostok have caused a severe cut back in shipping to Vladivostok." In a kind of vicious cycle, one of the causes of Vladivostok's congestion—but not the only one—was the distressful status of the railroads. And port congestion made it difficult to get needed equipment to those railroads.[33]

During 1919, in spite of the efforts of Colonel Stevens and the Russian Railway Service Corps, railroad facilities did not measurably improve, but they did remain a source of much hope, frustration, and international friction. In addition to "normal" problems of breakdown, supply shortages, and war, the line suffered from Russian corruption and, reportedly, Japanese obstructionism. Heid gave Stevens credit (admittedly before the fact) for any improvements when and if they came. He and other Americans clearly saw Stevens's successes or failures as inextricably tied to the success or failure of the Russian Bureau's and America's efforts to bring economic stability to Siberia.[34]

The United States remained firmly committed to supporting the work of Stevens's Russian Railway Service Corps. It was not always clear, however, just exactly who the Corps worked for. In negotiations with Japan, the State Department minimized the Corps's nationality:

> Mr. Stevens and his associates are the agents of the Russian people. The Russian Railway Service Corps will continue to be maintained from Russian funds at the disposal of the Russian Ambassador until such time as their service may be either continued or concluded by established authorities in Russia.

Lansing reiterated that the Corps's members were "agents of the Russian people" and, in Betty Unterberger's words, were "merely doing what [they] thought best for the Russian people in a spirit of unselfishness and disinterestedness." Thus, Americans had no qualms about championing Stevens as a nonpartisan head of the inter-Allied railroad committee finally agreed upon to jointly supervise the railroad.[35]

On the other hand, policy-makers made it clear, at least amongst themselves, that the Corps was helping to carry out American commitments in Russia. And when it finally left in 1922, it did so without any authorization one way or the other by any Russian officials. Writing in 1927, John Stevens bluntly asserted that the Corps stayed on after the armistice in order "to keep the [American] 'Open Door Policy' against our little brown brother and prevent him from grabbing the railroads." This raises images of the Corps as a kind of double agent, serving both Russia and the United States.[36]

There was very little ambiguity about the perceived importance of the railroad. In a policy briefing prior to his appearance before a congressional committee from which the State Department hoped to extract funding for the railroad, Frank Polk was told to "develop the strategic importance both from the point of view of Russia and of the United States of the Trans-Siberian Railway as being a principal means of access to and from the Russian people and as affording an opportunity for economic aid to Siberia." It was also suggested that he might mention "the potential value of this railroad as a means for developing American commerce." Eight months later, in September 1919, an American official in Siberia wrote the State Department that Russia's problem was not Bolshevism but hunger and that the Trans-Siberian was the country's "aorta" upon which everthing else depended: "The railway involves and overshadows the economic, financial and governmental activities" of Russia. It needed to be used to its full capacity—which unfortunately was not being done.[37]

Because transportation was a major bottleneck to economic contact between the United States and Russia, Americans, not surprisingly, objected to what they saw as Japanese disruption of American efforts to improve the rail system. Intervention had opened the way for Japanese military, political, and economic activities in Siberia on a grand scale. In October 1918 both Ambassador Morris and General Graves reported on the large number of Japanese troops and their apparent intentions to control the railroad. In November, on the eve of the armistice, the Russian Bureau's president, Vance McCormick, expressed concern that Japanese activities were hampering American efforts in Siberia, especially efforts to keep the railroad open. He argued that now that the German threat was ebbing, the United States should not allow Japan to take its place as another militaristic power oppressing the Russian people. On December 2, 1918, Lansing gave one explanation for American concern:

> This Government is concerned in the Siberian situation primarily because reports show that the paralysis of railway traffic created by the Japanese control of the Chinese Eastern and absorption of the railway for military purposes renders it impossible to furnish to the Russian population of Siberia the economic assistance which is vital to enable them to pass the winter without great misery and hardship. Furthermore the whole question of shipping supplies to the Russian and Czech forces in Siberia is imperilled.

Since Heid had made it clear that "great misery and hardship" were unlikely, Lansing may have been using this argument to restrain Japanese encroachments.[38]

While a great many variables influenced American policy making, one explanation for the continued postarmistice intervention was that the railroad would need protection if it were to be able to further its "beneficent effects of peace and trade." The Inter-Allied Railway Agreement between Japan and the United States implied that protection of the railroad was now the primary reason for continued troop presence. This agreement, arrived at in January 1919, was designed to foster cooperation in administering those sections of the line under their respective control. Writing of events covering the past several months, Frank Polk told the American delegation in Paris in May:

> I am ... trying to persuade the Japanese of the idea that the railway plan has altogether changed the situa-

tion since we sent out combined forces to rescue Czechs and steady the Russians; that everybody's business now is to restore the railways and emphasize the economic and constructive character of our undertaking and make the military side of it altogether subordinate.

Stevens, presumably representing the Russian interest, was named chief in-field executive officer, and the United States and Japan created a supervisory Inter-Allied Committee. The other Allies were invited to join in the agreement and the committee; by the summer of 1919 they had all done so.[39]

As of the spring of that year, most American policy-makers from the president on down were eager to keep the trains running and thought such a goal possible. The deplorable conditions on the road's physical equipment presented the most tangible obstacle. A great deal of capital investment would be needed or else the line would stop despite all efforts by the Railway Corps. Such an investment, if it could be made, would have a number of potential advantages. According to the Bureau of Foreign and Domestic Commerce, if the line could "be operated and transport satisfactory quantities of badly needed freight it will prove the greatest stabilizing influence." In furtherance of that goal, the plan creating the Inter-Allied Committee gave more control for the running of the line to the Allied committee and less to the Omsk Government—thereby breaking one logjam: the government had been obstructing westbound freight cars unless they contained military supplies or unless "huge sums" of graft changed hands. In April, Stevens reported that the shipments involved in the projected cooperative societies' sales "could not be handled at the present time" but that he hoped to be able to accommodate the transaction in a few months' time. In May the bureau told one interested American business that "there is a reasonable prospect that under the new [inter-Allied] control transportation inland will be possible on a considerable scale in about three months."[40]

Another purpose behind the Inter-Allied Committee was to provide funding to reequip the line. The four major participants (England, France, Japan, and the United States) each agreed to contribute approximately $5 million; the lesser partners paid in much smaller amounts if any at all. At all times it was assumed either that the railroad might begin to pay for itself and refund these moneys or that the expenditures would be reimbursed by a future Russian government.[41]

Where would America's share of this capital fund come from? With the conclusion of a peace treaty with Germany portending the dismantling of the War Trade Board and other war agencies and a return to tighter congressional controls and more rigid budgets, American officials spent much of April and May exploring methods of funding the railroad. The American peace delegation in Paris naïvely suggested that congressional appropriations would be readily forthcoming for money earmarked for an inter-Allied program. More politically attuned officials in Washington saw little hope of getting new appropriations passed through a budget-conscious Congress already skeptical of continued involvement in Russia. They resorted to a redirection of funds already allocated for use in Russia. This is where the Russian Bureau entered the picture.

In April 1919, with remarkably little discussion, the bureau "temporarily" loaned Stevens one million dollars of its capital fund for use on the railroad. It did so with the understanding that the bureau was assuming no responsibility for the railroad's operations. This was the first, and only, large scale expenditure of the bureau's capital. At almost exactly the same time this loan was approved the president had rejected bureau plans to loan money to the cooperative societies. It seems clear that he did indeed put a high priority on Russia's railroads. The loan is also evidence that exceptions could be made to the recall of "National Defense and Security" appropriations.[42]

In the end, the Russian Bureau provided all of America's $5 million share of the inter-Allied railway fund. It came from the $1 million loan and an additional $4 million of the Russian Bureau's capital fund which, when transferred to

State Department control, had Wilson's approval to be earmarked for use on the Russian railroads. At a May Russian Bureau board meeting, the directors noted almost in passing that the bureau "cannot hereafter use its funds to forward the purposes for which it was originally incorporated . . . and that it should therefore wind up its operations." This would make it possible to redirect money to what the directors apparently felt was the most pressing priority in Russia: funding of the railroad. They recommended the transfer of bureau funds "to use on the Trans-Siberian Railroad." One unsigned memorandum in support of using the bureau's capital to this end stated succinctly and forcefully that "The money presently involved [$5 million] is negligible in comparison with the benefits which will accrue to the United States as a result of the proposed loan to the Siberian Railways." Aware that the bureau had a short life expectancy in any case, and that improved transportation was vital to the economic health of Russia with or without an American government program of commercial assistance, the directors wanted the bureau's funds put to the best possible use in furthering its ultimate objective: helping Russia help itself through commerce.[43]

Such a transfer of governmental funds did require congressional approval, even though no new appropriation was involved. Recognizing the possibility of legislative hostility to continued involvement in Russia, Undersecretary of State William Phillips brought a number of arguments to bear in his defense of the transfer before the House Committee on Appropriations. First of all, the United States had already agreed to contribute to the Inter-Allied Committee fund, and to renege now would be extremely embarrassing in addition to being bad policy. Even more importantly, Phillips argued, the success of the forces of law and order in Siberia (and the consequent failure of the Bolsheviks) was dependent on adequate transportation. Failure to maintain such facilities would allow the further advance of "anarchy." Phillips also thought it worth noting that if order were not restored in Siberia American commercial interests would not be able to trade there. To prevent any misunderstandings, he assured the congressmen that this joint plan was not a donation, but merely a loan, which would be repaid "as soon as the economic life of Russia can be reconstituted." Since opposition to the "tide of Bolshevism" was by now an integral part of America's national defense, and since that was what these funds had been originally appropriated for, according to the undersecretary, Phillips hoped that Congress would see its way clear to making the necessary authorizations.[44]

This is one of the few times the Russian Bureau was overtly labeled as anti-Bolshevik in purpose and seems more accurate in hindsight than in original intent. It might be argued that the bureau had been antichaos or antianarchy in original intent—neither of which is ideologically linked to Bolshevism. But then Phillips spoke for the State Department's much more politicized and polemicized view of the world than for the bureau's own economic view of things. In any case, the United States Congress did not stop the State Department from using Russian Bureau funds to participate in the joint program to capitalize the Trans-Siberian.

Unfortunately, the money did not noticeably improve transportation services in time to serve America's purpose. Ironically, it may have served Russia's purposes.

In September 1919 the American representative on the Inter-Allied Committee to Supervise the Trans-Siberian split the blame for railroad difficulties equally between the Japanese and the anti-Bolshevik military in Siberia. He described how "food and other supplies have been allowed to deteriorate and spoil because it has been impossible to ship due to the claims of the Russian military that same might fall into Bolshevik hands. At the same time they would permit shipments to any district if enough money was paid them." The reasons for this sad state of affairs were, among others, personal disloyalty, dishonesty and corruption, and the Omsk government's obsession with military needs regardless of the plight of its people. The representative closed his report on a pessimistic note: "Conditions are deplorable and will rapidly grow intolerable as winter approaches. It is hopeless to expect Russians to cope with them."[45]

Nine months later the Russians—but the wrong Russians—were coping. In May 1920 a member of the Russian Railway Service Corps who had been held prisoner for a short time by the Bolsheviks reported that "The Siberian Railroad is now being run by the Bolsheviks better than at any time since he arrived in Russia. . . . [C]onditions are not disorganized or chaotic." On top of that, the line was successfully moving wheat into European Russia—which needed it desperately—and the engineer was impressed by both the military and civilian officials he had encountered. Quite conceivably, the Russian Bureau's $5 million had, in the form of new equipment captured by the Bolsheviks, helped make this possible. The Trans-Siberian was indeed being put to use to pull Russia together and help Russians help themselves —but not quite in the way Lansing, Stevens, and other Americans had envisioned.[46]

As of April 1919, however, the Trans-Siberian had not fallen to the Bolsheviks—nor had it received the Russian Bureau's capital fund. It is to that story that we now return.

The failure of American efforts to solve Russia's currency and transportation problems paralleled in time and in policy retrenchment the end of the War Trade Board of the U.S. Russian Bureau, Incorporated. At its May 16, 1919, meeting, the Russian Bureau's board of directors learned that President Wilson had sanctioned the bureau's dissolution.[47] It is not clear who actually made the first move in terminating the bureau or why it was made at just that time. McCormick and Wilson had yet to return from Paris, but peace with Germany seemed imminent and Wilson may have been making plans for the future. Had the peace treaty been ratified by the United States Senate without debate, America could theoretically have been at peace by July. All wartime agencies would have terminated at that point. Under such a scenario, the Russian Bureau's life was going to end soon anyway. The railroads needed the money as soon as possible. Perhaps policy-makers decided the advantages of having that $5 million reallocated before the actual conclusion of wartime authorizations outweighed any benefit two or three more months of bureau operations might entail. Wilson's evident unwillingness to spend bureau money either in loans or in direct commercial dealings also meant that its remaining bureaucratic and facilitator functions could be turned over to other, permanent government agencies.

In any case, at this May 16 and subsequent meetings the directors spent much of their time working out the technicalities of liquidating and transferring back to the federal government the bureau's assets and trying to ensure their reallocation to the Trans-Siberian. The directors did take time at the May 16 meeting to eulogize the bureau. As a kind of admission of its failure to live up to its potential, they noted that the most important services the bureau had been able to render had been primarily those of agent or administrator for other programs. The only "financial business transacted for its own account" had been the $1 million advance to Stevens, freight contracts with the Czechoslovak government for shipment of supplies to its troops, and the purchase of sample merchandise, some of which, unfortunately, had sunk en route and for which insurance would be received. The directors did not lay blame on anyone for the bureau's limited monetary involvement. They simply noted it as a reality.[48]

The May 29 board meeting set final allocation of the bureau's funds. With President Wilson's approval, the board agreed to turn back to the Treasury Department any unexpended balance from the bureau's capital fund on the expectation that the Treasury would then use that money to finance the United States government's participation in the Inter-Allied Committee to Supervise the Trans-Siberian. The sum thus reallocated was not, however, to exceed $4 million. (Adding the $1 million already loaned to Stevens, this would make America's contribution to the inter-Allied program $5 million.)[49]

On June 5, 1919, in compliance with the directors' decisions, the corporate existence of the War Trade Board of the

U.S. Russian Bureau, Incorporated, officially terminated. An executive order signed by Woodrow Wilson that same day authorized dissolution of the bureau as a government agency. During the last week of June 1919 all of the money over which the Russian Bureau had had control was ordered transferred from the bureau, through the Treasury Department, to arrive eventually at the State Department. The physical remnants of the Russian Bureau were moved into the State Department, which quickly divested carry-over operations of a separate bureau identity. The Russian Bureau as an agency specifically designed to encourage, through trade, Russia's economic rehabilitation, ceased to exist.[50]

Some tag ends needed attention before the bureau could be put to rest. It had some outstanding debts to pay and at the June 25 board meeting the directors resolved that the War Trade Board should be reimbursed for the bureau's expenses (salaries, supplies, cables, etc.) Much more interestingly, the bureau also had some profits to account for. Since the approximately $50,000 worth of sales handled by Heid on the bureau's own account was undertaken at a considerable loss, it is apparent that the bureau did not make its profit from that activity. Combined, the June 30, 1919, final operating report and the May 27, 1920, final report in liquidation, along with their balance sheets, provide an interesting perspective on the bureau's activities.[51]

The Russian Bureau received payments of approximately $735,000 from the operation of five ships under its control over and above the $765,000 it paid the War Department "in full settlement of cost of operating these five ships." Expenses incurred in transportation, in fees paid, and in reimbursement to the War Trade Board for operating expenses reduced the surplus to approximately $570,000. It does bear notice that a public corporation set up to provide economic relief to another country ended its approximately nine months of existence with more money than it had begun with. In point of fact, most of the profit came from other United States government agencies—the War Department and the U.S. Shipping Board among them—in freight payments for the use of bureau controlled ships.[52]

The final operating report also provides a picture of exactly what kinds of goods the bureau shipped. Of the original vessels assigned to the bureau, the users of their facilities included (in freight charge dollar amounts or tonnage): Czechoslovak military supplies (reimbursed through the Czechoslovak fund)—$304,000; the Russian embassy and the "Russian Mission of Ways of Communication" (the tag end of pre-Bolshevik Russia's supply operations headquarters in the United States)—$653,000; Standard Oil (kerosene)—$305,000; Katz Shoes—less than one ton; Bullard films—35 tons at $1,750; International Harvester—$35,000; Glushanok & Hill—$2,740; Pacific Steamship Company (for passenger privileges and slightly over one ton of stationery)—$12,220; miscellaneous small shipments at $50 per ton—$437,000. One ship carried railway material paid for by the Russian embassy at a gross shipping charge of $188,500. In this case the profits, by earlier agreement, were to be shared "equally between Shipping Board and Russian Bureau Incorporated."[53]

There was also the task of closing down the field offices. In Archangel, this basically meant bringing the Murmansk Fund activities to a close. The scope of Allied operations in northern Russia had been extensive enough to allow Cole to report, in April, that they could virtually fix food prices in the area. Prior to March 1919 the monetary value of supplies forwarded to the Archangel district was approximately $13 million, of which the American portion was approximately $4.4 million. About half this amount had been recouped through the sale of the supplies. In March an additional shipment had been made, thus depleting the American account. In April, the directors had authorized and the bureau had undertaken the purchasing and transporting of a shipment of seeds which, according to "urgent representations" from the American chargé d'affaires at Archangel, was desperately needed for spring planting in the northern provinces. Part of this cost had been paid by the "Provisional Government of the Northern Provinces" and the balance would be split three ways between the participating Allies and the United States. As of the May board of directors meeting, therefore, there was approximately $2.2 million in the fund, with the prospects for increasing that amount as sales revenues were actualized. Even though the core rationing program had been reduced to the shipment of flour only, the ongoing bookkeeping needs and the international commitments involved made it evident that some other government agency would have to take up administration of the program.[54]

An executive order dated June 24, 1919, had the Russian Bureau transfer to the State Department the current available reserves ($2,892,031.47) of the "Murmansk Fund." The department was authorized to continue using this fund for the civilian relief of "Russia or Siberia" and "including the necessary restoration of the railway traffic in Siberia." The State Department was also told that it had "been impossible" to finish off the administrative bookkeeping for the fund since there were accounts pending with other governments that would require adjustments and involve liabilities binding on the fund. The transfer, therefore, took place subject to any such obligations and the State Department would have to complete the bookkeeping itself when the "accounts pending" were cleared.[55]

The Murmansk Fund was handled separately from the bureau's own capital account in the June 1919 operating report. The original $5 million Murmansk Fund had been augmented by another approximately $1 million (part from the United States; part from England) to finance seed shipments. The listings of commodities purchased indicate contact with a large number of American firms in addition to the Food Administration Grain Corporation, which had to process the grain dealings. The Russian Bureau's final profit and loss statement did not include this fund, which showed a balance of almost $3 million on June 30, 1919, and was not included in the final accounting in May 1920.[56]

When the Russian Bureau closed, Felix Cole stayed on in Archangel simply resuming full time his original role in the consulate there. With the May withdrawal of American troops from northern Russia and the slow encroachment of

Bolshevik control in the area, he must have begun to feel somewhat isolated. In July Cole requested that at least one American ship remain in Archangel to dissuade Bolshevik propaganda about the United States deserting its friends and to mitigate feelings of having been "let down" among northern Russians. The Navy complied, leaving the *Des Moines* in port for the time being.[57]

Divesting August Heid of his bureau responsibilities took a little longer. In July he was told that his services would soon no longer be needed. McCormick cabled, a little prematurely it turned out, to thank him:

> No doubt by the time this cablegram reaches you all matters which you were handling for the War Trade Board of U.S. Russian Bureau Incorporated including Czechoslovak movement will be complete so far as your activities are concerned. I wish to take this opportunity to express both for the members of the War Trade Board and myself appreciation for the splendid service rendered by you in this work. I regret very much the change in policy which necessitated discontinuance of Russian Bureau activities.

Heid did not give up easily. When the War Department asked for his continued services in supervising its sale of goods to the cooperatives, he agreed and apparently took that opportunity to keep the Russian Bureau office open.[58]

On September 20, 1919, a cable from the State Department, telling Heid that the remnants of the entire War Trade Board were merging with the State Department and that all Russian Bureau activities were stopping, must have crossed an incoming cable from Heid announcing that deteriorating conditions in all fields precluded the continuation of relief measures and that he was closing up shop. Heid's is an interesting cable. It suggested that, in spite of all efforts to the contrary, as of September 1919 things were worse in Siberia than they had been a year before, when the bureau and Allied involvement in Russia first began. He mentioned, for example, the continuing rapid devaluation of currency and the increasing prevalence of Cossack martial rule by such men as the renegade Seminoff.[59]

Heid finally left Siberia in mid-December 1919. Shortly before going, he wrote a postscript to his experience with the Russian Bureau:

> So much of what the United States has undertaken for the Russians has been barren of immediate good results, so many potent anti-American influences are at work, and so much detail needs to be harmonized, that it requires a complete understanding between us to accomplish the results which were contemplated when this economic aid was proposed.[60]

In spite of all the foreign and domestic government and private sector expression of interest in trade with Russia and aid to Russia, the fact remained that very little commercial movement between Russia and the United States developed. A compilation of January 1919 figures indicated that export licenses for shipments to Vladivostok had totalled 4,400 tons of "miscellaneous merchandise valued" at about $3 million, not including supplies to the Omsk government and for the railroad. The figures for Archangel were 1,600 tons valued at $3 million and also comprised of "miscellaneous merchandise." Practically no import licenses had been issued, largely because the railroad facilities did not permit "material to arrive at Vladivostok from interior points."[61]

Detailed trade figures for 1918, 1919, and 1920 do not exist. The 1919 total of approximately $82 million far exceeded either the 1918 or 1920 totals and compared very favorably to the 1911–1914 prewar averages. This suggests that the bureau's efforts had some positive impact on private sector activities in Russia but, given the expectations and effort expended, the showing was not impressive.[62]

The complete understanding mentioned by Heid as a prerequisite to success had not been forthcoming—either between the government and the private sector or within the government itself. It can be argued that Woodrow Wilson never really knew just how he wanted to proceed in efforts to accomplish his desired Russian results and that this hesitancy, when combined with all the other obstacles to commerical relief efforts, doomed the program. The flaws, if there were flaws in Wilson's vision of restoring "revolutionary Russia" through commercial relief efforts, were not so much in execution as in planning.

Heid's departure from Vladivostok marked the end of the Russian Bureau as a functioning government program. It had not accomplished anywhere near what some may have envisioned early in the planning, but at least some of the problems had been beyond its control. The termination of this functional phase of the bureau's history did not, however, mean the end of conceptual plans to help Russia.

SIX

Relief Proposals, 1919-1920

The Russian Bureau as a functioning government agency faded from view quickly. The environment in which, and the ideas upon which, it had been founded did not disappear, although the 1917–1918 war atmosphere obviously had dissipated. There was even some talk of reorganizing and enlarging the bureau. But the last years of Woodrow Wilson's administration were not happy ones; the earlier optimism of creating a new world order gave way to a pessimistic and passive cynicism. Whatever Wilson and his advisers believed the future Russia would be, they had no choice but to recognize and deal with the present reality of a Bolshevik regime rapidly consolidating its hold over the nation. Policies aimed at revitalizing "revolutionary Russia" were, at best, piecemeal.

Wilson returned to Washington in June 1919 following the peace treaty signing. The War Trade Board and other

war bureaucracies prepared for their imminent dismantling. For the first time since June 1918 the vehemently
anti-Bolshevik State Department reemerged as the central
focus of both political and economic policy toward Russia. It
retroactively superimposed its own bias onto the Russian
Bureau in defending various positions and policies before
Congress, thus making it appear, to later observers, that the
economic relief effort had been primarily motivated by hostility to the Bolshevik regime. Wilson's preoccupation with
the Senate treaty debate and then his debilitating illness
meant that he exercised very little oversight over department rhetoric. The country's Russian policy suffered
through a period of presidential neglect just at the time
when frustrated officials at the State Department wanted to
take concrete action, in addition to rhetoric, to support the
anti-Bolshevik factions. Without Wilson's approval, however, no such action was forthcoming. By early 1920 the
anti-Bolshevik government in Siberia was in shambles and
all America's interventionist troops had been withdrawn.
Unable to save the sagging vestiges of revolutionary Russia
single-handedly, the United States significantly, if reluctantly, decreased its efforts, on all fronts, to help the Russians help themselves.[1]

Nineteen twenty witnessed personnel and personality
changes among the American policy-makers. Bainbridge
Colby replaced Lansing as Secretary of State. Frank Polk
and Breckinridge Long both resigned in June 1920; Basil
Miles had left earlier. New men filled these vacancies and,
however capable they may have been, they had not experienced the drama of diplomacy with revolutionary Russia.
Except for John Foster Dulles, few Russian Bureau staffers made the transition from the War Trade Board to
State Department employment. There was, consequently,
a major change in the personnel responsible for Russian
policy.[2]

Wilson himself changed after his illness. He became more
conservative, vituperative, and internationally skeptical.
According to historian Daniel Smith:

Now doubly embittered by his domestic frustration and the apparent willingness of America's co-belligerents to ignore her in determining the remaining details of the postwar settlement, Wilson seemed increasingly disillusioned and on occasion loath to play even that diminished role in European affairs still possible despite the Senate's failure to approve the Versailles Treaty.

On November 9, 1920, he wrote Colby a very negative letter about the "ugly disposition towards the United States of the four Powers now attempting to run the affairs of the world." By the end of Wilson's administration, the United States had cut many of its ties with these "other great Powers," whose cooperation would be vital in any further plans for Russia's salvation.[3]

During 1919 and 1920, press coverage of Russia continually gave the impression that the Bolshevik regime was in imminent danger of collapsing. According to Frederick Schuman, "Everywhere the figments of emigre hopes and imaginations were accepted as statements of fact." The reports Washington officials received reflected the confusion, the geographic variations, and the personal biases which had made evaluation of the Russian scene a difficult task from the beginning. As late as November 1920, an American in Vladivostok reported that "Prominent intelligent Russian tells me his private advices both Berline [sic] and Russia forecast early Soviet collapse." While these reports may have been very inaccurate, they were what Americans wanted to hear. And as long as a non-Bolshevik Russia seemed a viable option, ideas about helping such a Russia economically remained alive.[4]

The United States refused to recognize the Bolsheviks and, in fact, Wilson, writing in November 1920, blamed the Allies for their longevity: "As to Russia, I cannot but feel that Bolshevism would have burned out long ago if let alone." He was referring both to Allied political interference during intervention, which he thought drove nationalist Russians into the communist camp, and to British economic policy after 1919, which opened contacts with the Bolsheviks and gave them some, however limited, diplomatic legitimacy. The Wilson administration did continue to try to keep the Allies from pursuing policies which would bolster the Bolsheviks and impede the emergence of a progressive Russia.[5]

Wilson felt that any kind of contact, but especially commercial dealings, would simply provide the Bolsheviks with more opportunities to practice their preachings at home and in the larger world arena. He did not want to facilitate propaganda by providing the exchange media to finance international activities nor did he want to assist a reign of political oppression in Russia itself. Economic nonintercourse was the logical extension of nonrecognition and would help speed the Bolsheviks' political defeat. His eventual relaxation of trade restrictions resulted more from a realization that American nonintercourse would do little good if other countries did trade with the Soviets than from any fundamental change in thinking about the Bolsheviks.

When Wilson left office in early 1921 the Bolsheviks were still in power, the Russian Bureau was dead, American contacts with Russia had virtually disappeared, and yet the government's and the country's desire someday to help the Russians help themselves seemed to be in no way abated. In 1919, in the glow of a world peace conference, it had seemed more likely that forces both inside and outside Russia could initiate change. By 1920, America's ability to help would now have to depend more and more upon the Russian people themselves taking the first steps. Wilson left office still believing Bolshevism a temporary phenomenon, still expecting the true Russia to emerge in its stead. One might conclude, therefore, that the remarkable thing about American policy was not how it dealt with the Bolsheviks, but rather how it attempted to deal with Russia in spite of the Bolsheviks.

The dissolution of the Russian Bureau did not automatically mean that all American efforts to provide relief and assistance to Russia would also terminate. Although less prominent than in the days of the bureau, the concept of trade as a means of achieving anti-Bolshevik stability in Russia remained an ever-present element of policy and interest. It was, however, threatened by a "turncoat" tendency evinced by some Allied and some American initiatives to open trade with the "enemy," i.e., the Bolsheviks. The consolidation of Bolshevik control at least in western Russia further complicated the situation. The Supreme Council had, at the peace conference in mid-1919, established a blockade around Bolshevik Russia which, if the United States agreed to comply with the move, presumably precluded dealing directly with the Bolsheviks. But extensive areas outside Bolshevik lines, particularly in the west, continued in desperate need of assistance. America's post-Russian Bureau efforts at helping the Russians help themselves had to deal with the rapidly dwindling financial resources available to such efforts, and with the logistical problem of avoiding contact with the Bolsheviks. In eastern and southern Russia, assistance proposals continued to carry dual overtones of expanding American commerce and establishing a progressive, anti-Bolshevik Russia.

While never officially participating in the Supreme Council's blockade, the United States government supported it as much as possible. On November 4, 1919, in an open letter distributed to the press, Undersecretary of State William Phillips assured a hostile senator, leary of continued political efforts to influence events in Russia, that the United States was not engaged in any blockade of Soviet Russia. The government was simply not issuing any licenses or clearances for trade with Soviet Russia. This distinction may have been legally valid, but the results in each case were virtually identical. While not actually prohibiting trade (the blockade), it was not sanctioning trade (licensing). Having assured his readers that relief to non-Bolshevik areas of Russia would continue, Phillips explained the government's rationale for nonintercourse. Commercial dealings would make it easier for the Bolsheviks to finance propaganda campaigns in America and to further their goal of world revolution. The United States government also did not want to support and supply a "program of political oppression." Since the Bolshevik regime controlled all trade inside its territories, it would, of course, benefit from American economic activity there.[6]

Relief continued to areas in western Russia outside Bolshevik control for a while, but by the fall of 1919 the government's own funds to finance food shipments had been depleted. It now encouraged relief financed from other sources. Still thinking in terms of the "restoration of economic life in Russia upon [the] dissolution of [the] present regime," the State Department informed the Shipping Board in October 1919 that "It is the policy of this Department to facilitate in every way possible the delivery of food supplies to regions freed from Bolshevik control." When the Russian ambassador had difficulties processing a large purchase of grain, Wilson, from his sick bed, informed the United States wheat director that he, the president, considered "economic relief of this character" the "most effective means of limiting the spread of Bolshevism and of protecting, thereby, the Government of the United States from the dangers of subversive propaganda." He ordered the wheat director to "sell Russia the wheat, whether on credit or not."[7]

Most Americans probably thought the United States should help feed non-Bolshevik Russia. And most, but not all, agreed with the policy of avoiding all dealings with the Bolsheviks. In November 1919 an American military observer in Helsingfors reported his belief that "the present policy is a mistake." He wanted the United States to send food to Russia, dealing with the Soviet government as necessary while supervising the food's distribution and, in so doing, "try to cure Russia by lending a helping hand, rather than by the present starvation policy." Someone at the State Department labeled this "Hollyday's Credo." This "credo" bears some resemblance to the War Trade Board's earlier opposition to "economic strangulation."[8]

In January 1919 Ernest Harris, consul general in Siberia, had sent in a vehement indictment of all things Bolshevik.

Just one year later, he acknowledged Bolshevik supremacy
and dramatically altered his recommendations:

> I have come to the conclusion that the Bolsheviki are
> moderating from their position of terrorism and that
> wholesale executions and plunderings now no longer
> obtain.... I have no idea that one at all times can
> discuss with them any connecting plan, but I do believe
> that the time is come for us to get at very close range
> with them in order to study the situation.

Harris was expressing a modified, Siberian version of Hollyday's Credo, still not shared by many in the State Department.[9]

John Spargo may have been one reason so few in the State
Department favored that credo. By November 1919 he had
entered the lists of persons from outside government who
influenced the Wilson administration's conduct of Russian
policy. A rather soft socialist and erstwhile progressive re-
former, Spargo quickly assumed an anti-Bolshevik stand almost as vehement as Lansing's and became one of the most
overt exponents of using economics as a weapon against the
Bolsheviks. A strong economic nationalist as well as something of a political ideologue, Spargo began corresponding
with Lansing and may have had even more influence on
Colby. The substance of his November 4, 1919, letter to Lansing assumed that the Bolsheviks would shortly be overthrown and that Russia would establish a fairly liberal
constitutional government. Given that, Spargo wanted to
point out the upcoming vast material needs in Russia for
machinery and supplies, which he estimated to be in the
range of several billion dollars. "Shall this demand be met
by the United States, through the wise cooperation of her
capitalists and government, or shall it be left to the ordinary
chances of commerce, with the inevitable result that the
market will be seized upon by Germany and Japan working
in cooperation." If Germany and Japan did gain economic
control over Russia, Spargo was convinced that "No demo-

cratic nation will be safe or free to develop its own life." He
believed that the United States should secure a large share
of the Russian market, not for "exploitative purposes but to
help promote the emergence of a strong and free Russia,"
and consequently, of a strong and free international environment for democracy. Spargo closed this rather emotional
letter "respectfully" suggesting "that the Department of
State might well take the initiative in calling together a
group of American industrial and financial experts and others, for the purpose of considering the entire Russian situation and presenting at an early date a report with
recommendations for the guidance of the Government."
Spargo was afraid that left to their own devices American
businessmen would avoid the Russian quagmire (as in fact
they were doing) until it was too late both to open the door
and to save the Russians from exploitation. Consequently, he
wanted the government to assume an active role in encouraging and facilitating Russian-American trade, governments presumably being more attuned to long range
political and economic objectives than less visionary businessmen.[10]

Whether prompted by Spargo or by reopened State and
Commerce department discussions on the possibility, once
again, of sending some kind of American mission to Russia,
Secretary Lansing did devote much of November 1919 to the
preparation of a major proposal which he presented Wilson
in the first week of December. His suggestions illustrate that
many Americans, including many in the State Department,
still believed Russia could be saved and that America could
help.[11]

Lansing emphasized the importance of achieving an early
settlement of Russian "difficulties." Since that country
played a vital role in the world system of production and
distribution, it needed a government "capable of performing
its international obligations" and capable of keeping Russian resources away from renascent imperialists and "ad-
venturous revolutionaries, seeking to subvert democratic
governments everywhere." Lansing wanted a Russia free of

its leftist tyranny and able to assume its share of responsibility in a stable world order.[12]

He argued that the Bolsheviks remained in power only because of the "energy and ruthlessness which characterizes" their leaders, "the lethargy of large portions of the population" as a result of five years of war and nearly two years of famine and terror, and "the advantages inherent in a compact and central strategic position and the possession of the machinery of government," including the means of issuing paper money. While the White forces still faced obvious difficulties (Admiral Kolchak was in the throes of defeat as Lansing wrote this), the secretary was convinced that in the end they would triumph and that it was America's duty and obligation to "encourage by all available means the creation of a situation favorable to the rapid" achievement of that goal.[13]

Lansing thought America's future role in Russia would be primarily economic and that the time had come to put the whole Russian matter before Congress and to "obtain, if possible, the necessary legislation to aid in the economic rehabilitation of the Russian nation." After all, "unless Congress acts we will be helpless to continue [even] our present policy." Over the past year, Lansing wrote, the United States had adopted "every measure with respect to Russia which gave promise of hastening the end of civil war, the establishment of orderly constitutional government, and the relief of the material distress of the people." The success of those efforts had been restricted by legislation, by alternate demands on American resources, and by changing situations within Russia. Lansing did not include among the restrictions listed the government's own limited financial and participatory commitments. He did acknowledge that sending relief to people behind the Bolshevik lines might be one way of "fostering domestic peace and rational government" in Russia, but concluded that "all attempts in this direction have been frustrated so far by the uncompromising attitude of the Bolsheviki, their interference, for political ends, in the distribution of food and other commodities and their persistent attempts to avail themselves of any means to spread abroad their doctrine of violence and unreason." Obviously the Bolsheviks were obstructing a return to prosperity and rationality in Russia, but they were few in number and could conceivably be defeated militarily. Bolshevism, the more significant problem, and not restricted to Lenin's coterie, was "preeminently an economic and moral phenomenon against which economic and moral remedies alone will prevail."[14]

In line with the "vital need for relieving as soon as possible the economic distress which foments and perpetuates the popular state of mind called Bolshevism," Lansing proposed a threefold program. First, emergency relief in the form of food and supplies needed to be sent to Russia. He estimated that the cost would be $25 million and suggested that it could be administered and expended through none other than a revived bureaucratic Russian Bureau. Secondly, he recommended assistance of a more permanent nature to revitalize the normal processes of economic life. To that end, the railroad would be of primary importance. Approximately $15 million—to be "charged against the future Government of Russia" and ultimately recovered into the Treasury—was needed to assist the line. Finally, the secretary wanted to set up in the Trans-Siberian's service area, "as nearly a normal exchange of commodities as possible." A revived Russian Bureau, Incorporated, with a working capital of $100 million, would be established to facilitate this.[15]

Since the Bolsheviks were threatening the American way of life, it seemed only just, to Lansing, that America should take the struggle to the Bolsheviks and fight fire with economic fire. This was no simple cost-profit equation: "When the necessities of our self-defense call thus for measures which instincts of humanity and loyalty also dictate, there seems to be a manifest duty imposed upon the United States which it will perform with the same vigor and determination with which it has performed every duty in the past." For Lansing, there could be no better or clearer call to action.[16]

Lansing was now suggesting a $140 million expenditure to accomplish exactly the same goals Wilson had had difficulties appropriating $10 million for just a year earlier ($5 million to the Murmansk Fund; $5 million to the Russian Bureau and then the Trans-Siberian). Ironically, his $100 million suggestion for the corporate, commercial portion of a revived Russian Bureau was identical to that originally proposed by Secretary of Commerce Redfield. By November 1919 Lansing, for one, seems to have realized that America's original effort to help the Russians help themselves had been too little; his budgetary revisions came too late.

Lansing must have known that his program stood little chance of obtaining presidential, much less congressional, approval. Submitted while Wilson was recovering from his collapse and just before the secretary left office under a black cloud of Wilsonian disapproval, the proposal probably never even got serious consideration; certainly it never got implemented. On December 31, 1919, in response to an inquiry, Lansing had no choice but to say that the State Department (and thus the United States government) was currently "conducting no relief work in Russia or Siberia."[17]

If one uses the rather loose definition of "relief" as any form of economic intercourse, England still actively promoted Russia's economic recovery even if the United States did not. "Hollyday's Credo," which found little support in America, expressed ideas similar in nature to the direction British official policy was heading in 1920. During 1919 and especially 1920, the United States and England disagreed over Russia in general and trade with Russia in particular.

The withdrawal of American troops in northern Russia h .d been precipitated by just such disagreements. Friction with the British command and policies had caused the American troops to experience acute morale problems. In addition, Secretary of War Newton Baker felt that the troops were being used as a "cloak for the securing of concessions and commercial advantages" for the British. Wilson agreed that the situation was untenable. In late spring 1919, when the Arctic ports opened, these approximately 5,000 troops came home. They left behind one ship to discredit Bolshevik propaganda about America deserting its friends and to mitigate feelings of being "let down" among the local people.[18]

By 1920, Allied and American troop withdrawals and the White factions' defeats made chances for eradication of the Bolsheviks by military agents remote. The United States more and more focused its hopes on Bolshevism's defeat by nonmilitary pressure from the peoples it controlled. The best way outsiders could help was to make it as difficult as possible for the Bolsheviks to satisfy the needs and demands of these people. A certain amount of suffering for Russians now would be more than made up for by their salvation in the future. Here too, the United States and England disagreed.

The United States still followed its dual economic approach: encouragement of commerce—and thereby a return to normal conditions—in all those parts of Russia outside Bolshevik control, and a refusal to trade with those parts inside Bolshevik lines. But, whereas in 1918 and 1919 most of the Allies had been in agreement on such a dual approach, by 1920 a divergence of interests began to develop, especially between the United States and England. Woodrow Wilson still thought a strong unified Russia would provide an international marketplace that could foster human advancement everywhere. England, on the other hand, wanted a smaller Russia that would not threaten her empire but would still be capable of preserving the European balance of power. England did not hesitate, therefore, to deal with two Russias simultaneously: one Bolshevik, and one (or more) built from the territorial remnants of the White Forces.[19]

Given the 1919 and 1920 reality of expanded Bolshevik control, the British approach would seem, in hindsight, to be rather practical. But rumors of British recognition and/or trade agreements with the Bolsheviks displeased most Americans. Putting the darkest possible interpretation on British activities, Secretary Lansing hoped vainly that under the pressure of world opinion the British would "not dare to continue their selfish commercial policy." Lansing could see no purpose behind British contacts with the radicals other than "selfish commercial" advantage.[20]

In those areas of Russia outside Bolshevik control, Anglo-American difficulties reflected more purely commercial rivalry than political disagreement. Like the United States, England had an active governmental program to encourage trade. But unlike the United States, this program seems actually to have increased when the war ended, and evidence suggested a conscious collaboration between England's public and private sectors much stronger than America developed. For example, the British government offered risk insurance that protected businesses against almost any kind of loss in their dealings in Russia. A British firm reportedly had shipped $250 million worth of merchandise to south Russia. If accurate, that figure suggested a British trade far exceeding anything America could boast and highlighted the government's failure to induce American businessmen to compete in this seemingly promising market.[21]

The United States also failed to prevent England from changing its approach to the Soviet regime. By late 1919 England was ready to concede the reality of Bolshevik authority in part of Russia. British reassurances that no official relationship was contemplated did not completely relieve Lansing's disquiet, particularly when he learned that the Supreme Council had, in January 1920, announced an end to the blockade of Soviet Russia. Under British Prime Minister Lloyd George's leadership, the International Council of Premiers had decided that, with the White forces' defeats in Siberia and the western regions, trade now offered the best chance to destroy "the extreme reforms of Bolshevism in Russia itself" while actually strengthening Europe against vulnerability. Lloyd George said he had no intention of extending recognition to the Bolsheviks, but he did want peace with Russia. He thought the radicals were "changing color" and that opening trade "will bring about a stable regime." Not for the first time, economic expansion played a role in providing both the means and the ends in a policy rhetorically geared to political benefits. Rather cryptically, Lloyd George suggested that America's intransigence toward the

Soviets was "identical with that of Great Britain twelve months ago before vain expenditure of one hundred million pounds."[22]

Wilson did not accept this political rationale. He saw America and England "on the eve of a commercial war of the severest sort, and I am afraid that Great Britain will prove capable of as great commercial savagery as Germany has displayed for so many years in her competitive methods." Russia, in its disintegrated state, would be one site of this competition. Faced with active British promotion of relations with the Soviets, and unable to get Allied agreement on a common trade policy toward Russia, the United States began to loosen its own remaining trade restrictions. The State Department did not expect much actual trade to result nor did it expect recognition to follow. But private businesses would be free to trade in Russia, at their own risk.[23]

Wilson still had qualms about any contact with the Soviets even though it might now be the only way America could compete with "the monopolistic arrangements of the British for the control" of certain Russian products. The new secretary of state, Bainbridge Colby, was "very fearful that reopening channels of commerce might strengthen the Bolshevik war machine," which otherwise he expected to collapse by "July, more probably August" 1920.[24]

Nevertheless, partially because of British activities, the government officially lifted trade restrictions on July 7, 1920. Exchange restrictions remained in effect for another six months, however, and hindered any significant commercial intercourse. The lifting of trade restrictions should not be read as meaning the United States government had given up on its faith in the emergence of a progressive, non-Bolshevik Russia. Businessmen were warned that any concessions extracted from the Bolsheviks might not be binding on future Russian governments and that they were operating at their own risk and could expect no help from the government should they run into difficulties. Thus the political distinction made by American policy between Bolshevik and anti-Bolshevik Russia carried over into economic policy. England, which also made political distinctions between Russia's political factions, made fewer economic distinctions and was more willing to negotiate for commercial agreements with the Bolsheviks than was the United States.[25]

The United States government saw this as hypocritical opportunism and continued to object to Allied selfishness which threatened to benefit radicalism. The State Department tried to make it clear that America thought the Allies must desist from their imperialistic policies. In mid-August 1920, the American representative in Sevastopol reinforced this position when he reported British and French monopolization of trade in General Wrangel's territory and said that America's prestige ranked high throughout Russia because it was not associated with such opportunistic economic activities. Since America's abstention from economic opportunism came about in spite of (and not because of) government encouragement, there would seem to be some rather obvious ironies, if not outright hypocrisies, in the government's criticisms of British commercial success in Russia.[26]

All of this suspicion of the Allies and fear of trade opening up with the Bolsheviks was, from one perspective, a tempest in a teapot. In spite of early American fears to the contrary, the removal of the Allied blockade in January 1920 did not measurably increase Russian trade of whatever regional origin. And in spite of his negative view of French and British commercial activity in Russia, Woodrow Wilson could tell William Redfield's replacement as Secretary of Commerce that, as of May 1920, military intelligence reported very little actual trade between Europe and Russia. Thus the American fear of Bolshevism benefiting from commercial contact weighed more potently in concept than in reality.[27]

If the French and British activities in south Russia elevated America's prestige by contrast, such was not the perception of Japanese activities in Siberia. In pursuing its own self-interest, Japan damaged America's reputation while it took advantage of Russia's weakness. American observers saw the feared results of Japanese intervention solidify in 1919 and 1920. Instead of rallying to the interventionist forces or the White centers, large portions of the population looked to the "patriotic" Bolsheviks as the most externally uncorrupted Russian authority figures available. Many Americans blamed Japan for this impression. It seems clear that Russians were much more disconcerted by Japan's presence in Russia than by that of American or European forces. It also seems clear that Japan's activities were more disruptive than any of the other Allied participants. Not only did Japan's efforts retard the possible emergence of a progressive Russia but, because the United States had sanctioned the initial Japanese move, America's pronounced altruistic and sympathetic motives suffered some discredit.[28]

Throughout 1919 reports told of Japanese obstructionism prejudicing America's position, disrupting transportation, supporting Cossack brigands, and generally hindering efforts to bring stability to Siberia. There were also episodes of direct American-Japanese confrontation which caused some of the consular officers to fear possible military bilateral consequences. Indeed, the friction between America and Japan was so bad that in October 1919, when General Graves reported a possibility of Cossacks attacking American soldiers trying to protect the railroad and suggested that the Japanese would probably help the Cossacks "covertly at first, actively if necessary," a cabinet discussion (without Wilson in attendance) considered the possibility of full-scale war with Japan.[29]

Americans also feared that Japan might use its influence to gain economic control of eastern Russia. Banker Thomas Lamont wrote the State Department in June 1920 that "if Japanese General Staff is permitted to continue its present policy in Siberia we shall see that great region west [east?] of the Ural mountains in economic grips of Japan and most valuable market in the world closed to American manufacture and export."[30]

John Stevens lamented that "nothing but hell can be expected" from occupation of the railroads by Japan and its Cossack ally and documented renegade, Seminoff. Stevens informed the State Department that "I have labored for two years to keep these roads independent of a single outside control but the case seems hopeless." He therefore planned to pull his men out and come home. Colby asked him not to act precipitously, because a sudden departure would endanger American-Japanese negotiations over control of another, Chinese, branch of the railroad. In the end, the Russian Railway Service Corps stayed in Russia until 1922. While America's obvious concern about Russia's railroads was in part political and in part altruistic, it was also in part purely economic. Should the roads fall into Japanese control it would be virtually impossible for American businesses to penetrate the Russian market. At the same time, continued Japanese control in Siberia would undercut the political integrity of any Russian political force trying to reexert control.[31]

The Japanese finally left in 1922, partly in response to diplomatic pressures and partly in response to the spread of Red Army authority. While they remained, however, the Wilson administration found no way to solve its problems with Japan. All it could do was try to divorce itself from accountability for Japanese actions wherever possible and to avoid any contacts with Japan which could identify the United States with these actions. At the end of 1920 one member of the Inter-Allied Railway Committee to Supervise the Trans-Siberian reported that Russia was still "throttled by the Japanese and they have no intention of leaving here until the powers force them to go. No other nation can ever expect to have any trade here if they remain." Someone at the State Department underlined the last sentence. There is no way to know for certain whether the emphasis reflected American anxieties over lost American trade opportunities or Wilsonian frustrations over lost opportunities to help the Russians help themselves.[32]

The British, French, and Japanese activities in Russia, at least as perceived by American observers, clearly suggested that commercial opportunities did exist. But, unlike their international rivals, American businessmen showed—from the government's point of view—distressingly little inclination to take judicious advantage of them.

In September 1919, three months after Russian Bureau functions had been transferred to the State Department, Basil Miles circulated a memorandum highlighting Russia's continued economic and political importance. According to Miles, "the League of Nations practically ignores Russia," while both Germany and Japan were "devoting time, attention and money" to it. Pointing out Russia's size, population, and resources, Miles expressed dismay at the lack of serious interest being displayed "in regard to the greatest single problem bequeathed by the war." He suggested sending a "properly constituted commission" to south Russia, the Caucasus, and the Baltic Provinces, in addition to strengthening America's representation in Siberia—i.e., areas still outside Bolshevik control. Thus began a new round of suggestions for renewed America activity.[33]

Apparently in response to Miles, the department's Office of Foreign Trade Advisor prepared a memorandum highlighting obstacles to economic intercourse, specifically in south Russia. "The only self-interest appeal which could be made to [American businessmen] would be the suggestion that connections established now stand a strong chance of proving lucrative two or three years from now." Unlike the British, however, American businesses did not seem interested in "any projects involving deferred profits." Consequently, any American mission at that time would have to be either humanitarian or political, there being little economic incentive. It was the author's "personal view that the political reasons are very compelling" since this would facilitate development of an American sphere of influence "centered in Constantinople." Making it clear that he was thinking solely in terms of a private capital undertaking and not a government program, he suggested that if it were decided, from "political motives, to promote such a commission, it will be necessary for the Administration to make the matter a personal one with several leading businessmen." In other words, the government would have to take the lead in educating business to its long-term interests.[34]

That suggestion went for nought because the political staff of the State Department decided that any commission would have to be nonpolitical and motivated only by an interest in future trade. It was in light of these reports, and Spargo's urgings, and in awareness that the American private sector was showing little initiative of its own, that Secretary Lansing had suggested the revitalization of the Russian Bureau with a $100 million capitalization which would be able to prime the flow of trade between Russia and the United States enough that the private sector would take a closer look at Russia's commercial potential.[35]

But what future trade potential was there? The evidence tended to be conflicting. A November 1919 report indicated that the United States held a preferred position among influential Russians in the south. These men did not trust England; they needed America and wanted American help "because they believe Americans are true." The author thought abundant commercial markets existed in the area and the availability of exportable materials would make transactions relatively easy. Also in November the State Department was "encouraging in every proper way American firms which will undertake to trade with Siberia or South Russia. The need of the population in these regions for manufactured necessities is most pressing, and an out movement of Russian raw materials is, of course, the first step towards Russian economic recuperation." A December 1919 intelligence report suggested that American assistance to the White forces in south Russia would not only help bring stability and order to Russia but "would amply repay the United States in a commercial way in the not far distant future." Thus, there were indications that a commercial opportunity did exist which would also have beneficial political ramifications.[36]

On the other hand, Eliot Mears, U.S. Department of Commerce trade commissioner in Constantinople, reported at approximately the same time that "At the present time foreign trade in Azerbaijan is absolutely at a standstill. Little business can be done in the near future, due to the policies of the Government and the state of the currency." We have already noted Felix Cole's earlier hesitancy to promote trade in northern Russia because of the absence of any exportable materials necessary to compensate for the instability of ruble currency.[37]

These reports suggest that while in 1919 the government wanted to develop trade relations with non-Bolshevik Russia, the business community might well be expected to shy away from the risks involved. Nineteen twenty saw a reversal of government and business interests, with government encouragement decreasing in direct proportion to the increase in Bolshevik strength. With less and less territory still outside Bolshevik control, American diplomats recommended economic retrenchment. A report from Bucharest informed the State Department that "conditions are so uncertain [in Russia] that no one can accept orders or expect to be paid because the Russians have only roubles. It would be advisable to make the American public acquainted" with these conditions. Ironically, this report was prompted by the increasing number of Americans traveling to Odessa, presumably in search of trade opportunities. Some American firms still had representatives and even offices in Russia, particularly in Siberia. In the spring of 1920 Bolshevik expansion into the area prompted the consul in Vladivostok to counsel retrenchment or termination of business activities at least until the situation returned to "normal."[38]

By the summer of 1920, even though the United States government had lifted trade restrictions, it was discouraging contact or commerce with Russia—a term now used even in official correspondence to mean Bolshevik Russia. The chargé d'affaires in Helsingfors cabled that "American businessmen should be warned to place absolutely no confidence in contracts with Russia or Esthonia other than those providing for payment in advance by confirmed bankers credits in America and actual payment against shipping documents only." The government rejected all responsibility for persons traveling in Soviet Russia and informed the public that it would provide no assistance in any dealings which might involve the Soviet regime. In response to reports of commercial opportunities in Bolshevik-controlled Vladivostok, an

October 1920 Office of Foreign Trade Advisor memorandum
read:

> Smith is over-optimistic about the guarantees of the
> Russian government in Vladivostok. I would not recom-
> mend any American business man to accept such a
> guarantee nor even suggest that American ships stop
> at Vladivostok. . . . The importance of the "gateway" of
> Vladivostok cannot be over-emphasized, but it cannot
> be kept open at the expense of American business
> which has lost millions through the requisitioning
> habit of the Vladivostok Government.

The State Department was actively downplaying possible
commercial opportunities brought to its attention by its own
field representatives, simply because the area involved was
no longer free of Bolshevik influence.[39]

On the other hand, private commercial interest in Russia
increased in 1920. As the postwar recession in America continued, Warren G. Harding's campaign and election gave the
State Department some difficult months during which it was
flooded with reports of Harding's receptivity to trading with
the Bolsheviks, and of Bolshevik anticipation of a relaxation
once the new administration was in office. Apparently businessmen were responding favorably to the relative stability
returning to Russia under Bolshevik rule regardless of that
regime's ideological bent.[40]

John Spargo, a staunch advocate of nonintercourse with
the Bolsheviks, did get the government to issue a statement
aimed at preventing any alteration of America's political
and economic policy toward the Soviets as a result of Harding's election. Although he got the statement he wanted, it
is beyond the scope of this study to explore the development
of trade relations under the incoming Republican administration.

It is within this study's scope to restate the actual trade
statistics for the years of Wilson's efforts toward revolutionary Russia. According to the Committee on Russian-Ameri-

can Relations' research in the early 1930s, the figures for 1918–1920 were: in 1918, exports to Russia $17,335,518, imports from Russia $10,760,007; in 1919, exports $82,436,185, imports, $9,663,088; in 1920, exports $28,727,718, imports $12,480,586. These figures compare with a 1919–1914 export average of about $26,000,000 and a 1916–1917 wartime export average of about $440,000,000.[41]

These raw statistics do suggest that the Russian Bureau may have increased exports to Russia during its relatively short lifespan. Eighty-two million dollars was not, however, going to rehabilitate four years and more of devastation and depletion in Russia. The figures also suggest, as Heid had implied, that Russia did not have enough exportable commodities to prevent a significant trade deficit in its overall balance sheet. And finally, the evidence implies that Bolshevik victories, coupled with a drop in government enthusiasm, produced a decline in American sales to Russia in 1920—a decline, that is, from the halcyon days of the war years and from 1919. The 1920 figures were not a decline from the prewar averages. Russia's March revolution, with its democratic overtones in a country of impressive economic potential, may have begun a "Russia market" myth analogous to America's longtime, but basically unrequited love affair with the China market. Perhaps the United States was simply never destined to save Russia from itself or create an Open Door in Russia for its surplus goods.

But, as has been true with China for so long, it was very hard to convince Americans of their limitations in Russia. On December 23, 1920, an American agricultural expert who had spent the last two years observing conditions in and relaying information about eastern Russia to the State, Commerce, and Agriculture departments, submitted his final report. Charles Tuck did not agree with the official policy of isolating Russia economically. Every effort short of recognition should be made to facilitate and encourage American trade in and around Russia. He thought the Red Cross and other relief societies were discriminating against Russia and he wanted them to reverse that policy and render relief to all classes regardless of their political affiliations. Tuck was another believer in Hollyday's Credo. Tuck closed his report with a recommendation that was hardly new. He proposed that a commission, composed of diplomatic, business, and agricultural advisers, be established capable of supplying information on all activities in Russia and, in the future, of coordinating and administering the agricultural and industrial assistance that a recognized, progressive Russia would need in its reconstruction. Like others before him, Tuck thought a prospering economy would draw people away from Bolshevism, expunge the physical conditions which fed the disease, and rid Russia and perhaps the world of this ideological threat to order and stability. And like others before him, Tuck wanted the United States to play a major role in bringing about the salvation of revolutionary Russia.[42]

SEVEN

Conclusion:
Wilson and Russia

The War Trade Board of the U.S. Russian Bureau, Incorporated, had been designed to facilitate the expanded trade relations with Russia which many Americans hoped would bring out Russia's progressive, democratic potential. The bureau failed to promote extensive trade; Russia succumbed to radical Bolshevism. Both these results may reflect less on the bureau's own execution of its program than on the policy concepts of Woodrow Wilson and his advisers.

If one assumes that the correlation between extensive trade and the emergence of a progressive Russia would have been direct and unequivocal, scholarly inquiries could be limited to finding reasons for the bureau's failure to induce large-scale trade relations. If, however, the directness of that correlation is in doubt, as in my opinion it is, then other questions need to be looked at as well. Among others, such questions would include an analysis of just exactly what

Wilson wanted to do, at given times, and what priorities he imposed on the limited resources available. Did he want to help the Russians—or hurt the Bolsheviks? Did winning the war, or restraining the Allies, or fulfilling his own principles take priority over helping the Russians? How far was he willing to use the government? What kind of relationship did he realistically expect between government and private sector efforts in Russia? There seems good reason to argue that Wilson and many of his advisers never really looked too closely into these interrelated issues. Instead, they assumed that all the various goals and participants would work together to everyone's advantage. This is what I would call a conceptual shortcoming.

Taking first things first, why did the Russian Bureau fail to promote extensive Russian-American trade? And given that overriding reality, what conclusions can be reached about the bureau's operations?

When it came time to close the Russian Bureau's records, a retroactive lowering of expectations emerged. According to the last operating report, that of June 30, 1919, the bureau's purposes had been less ambitious than those, for example, suggested by the press release cited at the beginning of this study. Now the objective was "mainly the purchase and shipping of supplies of food, clothing and necessary implements for purchase by the Russian people in Siberia and Russia and for the purpose of maintaining cordial relations with the Russians." Direct government involvement was explained "because private traders, in view of unsettled conditions, were unwilling to assume the risks incident to shipping merchandise to these localities." There was little of the earlier rhetoric of helping Russia help herself or of assisting in the rehabilitation of Russia's economic life. The distinctions may seem minor, but they reflect the bureau as it actually functioned rather than the earlier ambitions for a bureau that perhaps never could have been. By 1919, Americans had recognized that their efforts constituted more a gesture of support than an actual contribution to reconstruction. The June report also incorporated support to Stevens and the railroad as one of the bureau's primary contributions to Russia. Emphasis on the railroad reflects what actually happened—perhaps the most important thing that happened—to Russian Bureau funds rather than what had originally been intended for those moneys.[1]

The scope of American assistance to revolutionary Russia envisioned by S. R. Bertram, or Cyrus McCormick, or Basil Miles, in late 1917 and early 1918 was simply never achieved. The hundreds of men and millions of dollars needed to induce a political and spiritual "rebirth" of democratic Russia never came into play. As a result, the program had little chance to achieve the goals some of its initiators had hoped for.

There are several possible explanations for this expectation-performance gap. New to the game of foreign assistance, the government did not know how much "pump priming" would be needed to produce a healthy flow of private sector trade. Wilson seems to have been particularly tight-fisted fiscally. Very few Americans fully comprehended the obstacles to trade presented in a war-torn and financially chaotic Russia. Planners did not always understand domestic realities. Heid may well have thought the men in Washington naïve in their expectations of instant trade. Those same men were equally doubtful of the Paris delegation's naïve assumptions about America's domestic receptivity to Wilsonian goals. Government officials also overestimated private sector enthusiasm.

The timing was bad. The program began in the winter, long after Russia's harvests. In Siberia, both Morris and Heid suggested from the beginning that not much could happen until at least spring—and by spring the bureau was dying. In northern Russia, frozen port facilities discouraged trade.

The hazy relationship between government and private sector responsibilities was further blurred by some confusion over whether the bureau's primary task was to help Russia or help American business. As soon as trade restrictions and controls were eased, the bureau backed off, leaving

Russia's needs to be satisfied by a private sector unwilling to take chances. The cooperative society sales suggest that Russia had ready customers, but only the War Department and the bureau were ready to risk financing such sales.

On the other hand, Woodrow Wilson never gave any indication that he expected more from the bureau than what he got. The bureau served the United States government well as a coordinator of programs. It had propagandistic value as a symbol of American concern and American willingness to help. But it was clear from the beginning that the help would come only if Russia was willing and able to help itself. Outsiders could not "force" salvation. Wilson expected the private sector to take much of the responsibility for improving trade relations. From that perspective, he may have been disappointed in the private sector while at the same time perfectly satisfied that the bureau had done all it could. There was little Wilson could do about the Russian reactions.

Viewed from a practical perspective, the Russian Bureau operated within very definite limits. Under any circumstances, and using however much money, the United States was also limited in what it could have done to save Russia.

The accountants had a rather easy time with the bureau's final financial balance sheets. The same may not hold for its performance record. The bureau had, in the beginning, a number of clearly spelled out purposes: domestically, it was to serve as a clearing house for information on and coordination of all Russian activities; in the field, it was to serve as a source of economic relief, to facilitate the growth of Russian-American commerce (seen as another form of relief), and to work to stabilize the economy and thereby help the Russians reconstruct their economy and consequently their national polity.

The bureau did serve as a source of information. It did provide American business with a great deal of data relating to economic opportunities. But it never seems to have become well enough known to eliminate a flood of inquiries coming to the Department of Commerce rather than to the bureau. It did provide the government with some of the most trustworthy reporting on conditions in Russia. It did not, however, become the clearing house at one time envisioned, either for information or for policy. This may have been less the bureau's fault than a result of bureaucratic intransigence elsewhere and the early armistice, which gave the bureau something of an impermanent atmosphere and thereby militated against using it as a center for long-term planning. The State Department, having to deal with a wide variety of Russian issues, developed a Russian Division even as the bureau was being established; the Department of Commerce also opened a Russian division in early 1919. The paper record does not indicate much coordination between these three agencies. The Russian Bureau simply was not old enough at the time of the armistice to have established itself as the focus of things Russian. By mid-1919 it would be easy for the State Department to assume that role, especially with Redfield no longer at the Commerce Department, House no longer having the president's ear, and the remnants of the War Trade Board itself having been merged with the department.

As a source of relief, the Russian Bureau's balance sheet is lopsided depending on location. The Murmansk Fund delivered food to northern Russia, which did not survive long free of Bolshevik control once the program and the troops left. On the other hand, the bureau inherited that program—as opposed to having initiated it—and, given the inter-Allied aspects involved, some other agency would undoubtedly have administered it had the bureau never existed. In any case, the Murmansk Fund involved none of the bureau's own capital. In Siberia, the bureau expended very little of its own money in the procurement of relief. Heid saw no major need for "emergency" relief and would not or could not, depending on the time frame, use government money to engage in nonemergency trade. The bureau did facilitate Red Cross and other nongovernmental traditional relief efforts, and it did encourage some direct trading.

The negotiations over sales to cooperatives must fit somewhere between providing traditional relief and facilitating Russian-American commerce. Using bureau funds to finance the American involvement in the Inter-Allied Committee to Supervise the Trans-Siberian also fails to fit precisely into one of the original categories of purpose, although it obviously related to the expectation that improved railroad transportation would greatly increase the chances of economic reconstructive success.

The bureau worked hard to encourage the development of Russian-American commerce but had little success to show for its efforts. Currency and transportation problems and the general instability in Russia—all far outside its singular control—were major reasons for the poor record. The American private sector's hesitancy presented an equally fatal barrier to trade.

Of its broadest, almost rhetorical purposes, the bureau did very little to bring about economic stability and consequently "help the Russians to help themselves." This shortcoming must be credited in part to the bureau's architects and in part to conditions well beyond American control. But the bureau's operations were also hampered, from the beginning, by hesitancy within and opposition without the government. Wilson flatly rejected Redfield's $100 million figure—which in retrospect may have been much nearer the mark than the $5 million actually authorized; the bureau staff both in Washington and in the field seemed reluctant to spend even that small sum. The private sector, while happy to receive information and have support work done for it, simply did not follow through on opportunities. It also resented government regulations on one hand and the perceived threat of government competition on the other.

Although N. Gordon Levin sees Wilsonian activities such as the Russian Bureau as a kind of "proto-Marshall plan,"[2] in fact the bureau, unlike the Marshall plan, was a very reluctant government undertaking with so small a monetary commitment but so elevated a rhetoric that almost nobody was happy with the results. And unlike later American foreign aid programs, it distributed no grants of money. The Russian Bureau never gave anything to anybody. However much Wilson wanted to help the Russians help themselves, he refused to put much government clout into the crusade. The shortage of shipping space also indicates a certain hesitancy of commitment. Wilson could, at any time, have ordered the transfer of more vessels to Pacific duty—but he apparently deemed their war use in the Atlantic more important. Again, when business did not find conditions conducive, rather than undertake commercial relations on its own, the government simply withdrew.

There are, of course, a number of reasons explaining that withdrawal above and beyond Wilson's hesitancy to make a major financial or resource commitment. On a rather mundane level, the legislative demise of the War Trade Board carried with it the demise of the bureau as originally and bureaucratically conceived. When transferred to the State Department, it had virtually no capital funds remaining and was quickly subsumed by the interests and orientation of the much more political department which, additionally, already had its own representatives in the field. If it had continued to operate, under whatever bureaucratic umbrella, the bureau would have had funding difficulties. Once the war ended, Congress would probably not have sanctioned a major expenditure no matter what the projected private sector returns might eventually be or what the political implications for Russia might be. The private sector would have objected vociferously to government expenditures which today might be called pump priming but which then would probably have been seen as a kind of socialism. According to Joan Hoff Wilson, by 1920 the private sector encouraged government participation in investments such as the Chinese consortium efforts[3]—although the government itself remained reluctant—but it indicated no desire to have government participate in commerce per se.

The transportation and currency difficulties that plagued Russia also prevented extensive commercial interaction, whether governmental or private, just as most observers in the field had suggested they would. More generally, the quixotic conditions in Russia simply did not bode well for a massive economic assistance program however constructed if, as seems to have been the case both for government and business, that program was premised on no loss of money and on operating in a stable environment.

In summary, the Russian Bureau provided too little, and did even that too late. Whether massive infusions of relief earlier could have overcome Russia's internal problems is a moot, but admittedly intriguing, question. The even more intriguing question is whether a modified version of Hollyday's Credo—whereby relief was administered in Bolshevik as well as non-Bolshevik regions—might have changed the course of Russia's revolution. That kind of policy hypothesizing relates not to the bureau's actual performance record but to its larger policy and perceptional environment.

The Russian Bureau, it must be remembered, operated within the constraints of Woodrow Wilson's global vision of Russia and of the world. One reason for the rather early withdrawal from America's economic adventure in Russia may have been the multiplicity of seemingly more pressing world events. Since almost everybody saw the Bolsheviks as a temporary, if disreputable, phenomenon, they understandably put priority on tackling the not so temporary ills of the world. When Russia came to its senses, as assuredly it would eventually do with or without Russian Bureau assistance, then it could be fitted into an orderly world *assuming* that a League of Nations existed to structure that order. On a priority scale, therefore, the League ranked much higher because it formed the glue to hold the puzzle—in which Russia, or any other country, or any government agency was but one of the pieces—together.

The same kind of reasoning can be applied to Bolshevism, which seemed much more of a threat if manifested in Germany or England than in Russia. Isolate the original source, yes, but be more immediately worried about preventing its infectious spread.

Wilson's policy toward Russia itself offers an analytical challenge. Criticisms which seem warranted from a 1980s perspective may do injustice to the intentions of the policy formulators and to the circumstances of the policy's formulation. The world, after all, looked very different in the 1980s than it did in 1919.

Post-tsarist Russia was unique. It witnessed one of the most unsettling events in world history. American policy makers had few precedents on which to pattern their reactions. They had already internalized expectations based on their interpretation of Russia's March revolution. The Bolshevik takeover found no place in this picture. Rather than change their expectations, Americans groped in the dark for an intangible creation of their own minds.

At the same time, by the end of the war, the United States had become interlocked with the world in such a way that even the pique of a strong executive could not extricate it. If the policy-makers of that day made mistakes in their handling of the Russian situation, they had the justification of ignorance about, and inexperience in, their position of power and responsibility.

Most of Woodrow Wilson's foreign policy was based on ideological expectations rather than on a conscious concept of the judicious exercise of power. He expected citizens and corporations both to do their share in overcoming the intransigence and treachery of power-hungry governments. Presumably, all the people would need would be moral encouragement supplemented by very minor amounts of material support. Businesses would be eager to spread progressive democracy through expanded trade. When the people and the businesses did not respond—as they did not in Russia and probably could not realistically have been expected to—Wilson was more inclined to pout or sermonize than to take action.

Government's self-image also had not kept pace with the changing world. The American philosophy of government was only just beginning to explore public regulation of private capital as a part of its responsibilities outside wartime emergencies. Even the most progressive of America's leadership held firm to a concept of fiscal responsibility which in the world of Keynesian economics has become associated with the most conservative dogmas. The Russian Bureau represented a major departure from precedent in that Wilson allotted government money to undertake a task normally delegated and reserved to private business. It was, however, a wartime agency and Wilson would not make a large enough commitment even during the war to begin to accomplish his goals. That he even tried is indicative of how strongly he felt about his entire Russian ideal. That his efforts, at least in retrospect, seem rather halfhearted is indicative of how hesitant he was about the proper means to achieve those goals.

Wilson's foreign policy advisers were not in the best of all positions to help him launch new departures in policy. The State Department had not yet adjusted to twentieth-century diplomatic requirements. The network of informational sources and professionally trained staff which is the modern department was not the department of Lansing or Colby. Foreign policy formulators often worked under conditions of informational ignorance and operational obsolescence. Most of these men, however innately intelligent, did not have the level of familiarity, the firsthand experience, or the textbook historical training desirable in making major, long-term decisions about Russia. The field representatives had no training to prepare them for the analytical and insightful diplomatic reporting which it now fell their duty to perform. With a few exceptions, even the most highly qualified and perceptive of America's representatives in revolutionary Russia were confounded by their environment.

The Russian Bureau staff, and most notably its directors, seem to have been less ideologically blinded than the State Department on one, political, level, and perhaps even more so on another, economic, level. Thus the bureau counseled retrenchment when there was even a remote, hypothetical chance of competing with the private sector. But the bureau also disagreed with Wilson and the State Department's policy of economic strangulation. Siberia did not provide much ground during 1918–1919 on which to test "Hollyday's Credo," but it was (and is still today) interesting to hypothesize about what might have been the result had America and the Allies tried to "kill Bolshevism with kindness" rather than isolate it into dogmatic and reactive inflexibility. Had such a course been tried, the Russian Bureau personnel would have been much better suited to its implementation than would the State Department. For example, Heid's reports tended to be fairly objective analyses of economic conditions, and he saw the Kolchak regime in its true, rather unimpressive light. Such cannot be said, in general, for the sometimes fanatically anti-Bolshevik consular reports. As noted earlier, Felix Cole, a consul himself, was not immune to the political bias bug.

Personalities and personnel aside, there is always the question of how much influence the United States could have had on Russia's future under any circumstances. Rather cynically, in early 1920 the contemporary Russian expert George Kennan acknowledged that it was too late to try to help Russia, but he clearly believed that the United States could have done so earlier. Particularly disgruntled about the sparsity of military activity, Kennan wrote: "We had a wonderful chance in Siberia but we lost it through irresolution, weakness, and a deplorable misunderstanding of the Russian character and the Russian situation." He did not necessarily blame the State Department, noting that it had "probably" done the "best it could under paralyzing conditions." It is less clear just exactly who Kennan did blame.[4]

Woodrow Wilson and George Kennan may both have been wrong—as Americans often were in their evaluation and interpretation of things Russian—both because of misperception and because of insufficient and inaccurate information. Wilson was searching for a democratic Russia which he firmly believed to be a genetic characteristic of those two hundred odd million people. That Russia may simply never have existed, and the United States may, consequently, have been impotent to guide the Russian people into a United States of Russia.

At the same time, there can be no doubt that Wilson was motivated by a sincere concern for Russia. The concern was genuine and frequently altruistic as international politics goes. He wanted a Russia ideologically compatible with, if not everything American, at least the progressive democratic trend Wilson foresaw as the road of the future. And he wanted that not because it would make Russia a better friend of the United States, although presumably it would do so, but because that road was the best course for mankind everywhere. His policies were, therefore, more open to criticism than his ideals.

Wilson's nonrecognition of the Bolsheviks meant much more than a simple withholding of a ritualistic diplomatic honor. The policy precluded American efforts to modify the very ideology it feared so much by working from within the Bolshevik structure, working with Russia in spite of the Bolshevik structure. The United States government's rejection of Bolshevism, ironically, meant that it would become impossible to help the Russians help themselves. America did not, for example, follow through on its own food policy rationale, which suggested logically that a massive influx of food—regardless of who distributed it—would undercut Bolshevism's hold on the population by eliminating the conditions which Americans believed had produced that hold. Wilson rejected the possibility, suggested by some of his own advisers and by the British after 1919, of at least trying to deradicalize Bolshevik Russia through outside contact.

Had he accepted the possibility, he had in the Russian Bureau a ready-made vehicle for such an undertaking. Recognition would have served to legitimize, if not actually stabilize, the currency dealings necessary for any Russian-American trade, and it would have given American firms much more confidence in undertaking commercial ventures in Russia. The bureau could have engaged in transactions in its own right or simply done what it had been doing—facilitating private sector contacts. In either case, a significant amount of commercial intercourse might have developed—thereby expanding American foreign trade and giving Wilson a chance to test his belief that commerce and prosperity would lead toward the democratization of Russia.

For purposes of analysis it really doesn't matter whether Wilson's theory was right or wrong. He boxed himself out of any significant role in determining Russia's future should that future develop in a Bolshevik context. Had America tried to exert a moderating influence directly on the Bolsheviks, the tangible results, even in total failure, could not have been much worse than those obtained through the course he actually pursued.

Even accepting the validity of Wilson's policy of economic strangulation, one wonders why the relief program to non-Bolshevik Russia was so closely tied to war and so quickly cut off in peace. If Bolshevism was worth fighting, and/or a revolutionary Russia worth pursuing, surely this was as true in peace as in war. In all honest probability, Congress would not have authorized continued Russian Bureau activities. But the point here is that the administration never really tried. It never even asked Congress for continuation appropriations. It readily accepted, in very atypical times, the typical wartime/peacetime dichotomy between accepted kinds of government activity. One has trouble imagining a modern day "imperial" presidency being so completely hamstrung by Congressional hostility. And perhaps it bears note that two years later the Harding administration obtained huge appropriations for famine relief to Soviet Russia.

Criticisms such as those already mentioned tend, in a cynic's mind at least, to raise questions about the level of Wilson's commitment to Russia. Was he more interested in projecting an image as altruistic world leader and friend of democracy than in making a realistic effort to help the Russians? Were his efforts to restrain Allied exploitation of Russia designed to help Russia, to leave the field more open to American penetration, or simply to protect the Allies from their own unfortunate proclivities? Wilson did try to limit Allied activities. He showed a sincere concern for how the world conducted itself and for the preservation of Russia as an independent, unfettered national entity. But in his own behavior Wilson exhibited an almost sanctimonious self-righteousness and grandeur of vision which made his policy, however restrained, almost as difficult to justify as the overt violations of France, England, and Japan. Wilson, of course, would not have agreed. He distinguished between the exercise of influence directed toward fundamental social reform and influence exerted primarily to benefit oneself. He did not, for instance, consider America's mutually beneficial economic plans to restructure Russia's social and political reality through capitalism a form of interference. To him, America was only assisting in the natural unfolding of Russia's democratic tradition, acting as the agent of humanity as it were. America's economic plans, because they would spread the liberalizing influence of democratic capitalism, were inherently and unquestionably "good." England's political and economic maneuverings were "bad" because they did not fit within a Wilsonian pattern of human development, because they reflected a diplomacy of intrigue rather than honesty, and because they looked to benefit England above all else. An element of evangelical obtuseness emerges from Wilsonian America's repeated insistence that the United States was the only disinterested party and that American interference economically was not really interference and not really self-interest but rather the good samaritan deeds of a prophet nation.

Clearly, Wilson believed that economic efforts such as those by the Russian Bureau fell into this beneficial class. A two-sided coin, commercial expansion into Russia would obviously be in America's economic interest, but it would also redound to Russia's and the world's benefit. Capitalism, after all, was believed to be the mother of democracy. There was a "kicker," because the expansion needed to be "open door" capitalism or else the emergence of spheres of economic interest could spell exploitative imperialism and/or repressive socialism instead of democracy. Thus the United States resented and resisted Japan's inroads in Siberia and feared England's negotiations with the Soviets.

It is, of course, misleading to generalize about "America." Much of the economic ideology discussed in this study may apply more legitimately only to Wilson and Wilsonians. But Joan Hoff Wilson has credited the businessmen of the day with similar sentiments, at least as regards capitalism and democracy.[5] When the United States Government dropped its economic activities in Russia, it does not necessarily follow that all Americans had given up on helping in the emergence of a progressive Russia. The private businessmen who continued to explore commercial opportunities—with the Soviets as well as the anti-Bolsheviks—believed their efforts would help instill democratic, progressive impulses in Russia as well as net themselves a financial profit.

Wilson the peacemaker boxed himself in because of and in spite of his suspicions of the Allies, by taking ambivalent stances on whether to function singly or jointly in Russia. His ambivalence reflected an inability to decide whether other nations of the world were or were not trustworthy. One of the conclusions that must be drawn is that Wilson saw the world through a peculiarly distorting lens. He held to an idealistic vision of some projected goal long after the reality had taken root and was thriving. Stephen Bonsal quoted George Clemenceau as saying, during the Paris Peace Conference:

> Tonight I am depressed. I fear we shall never attain the world situation that Mr. Wilson seeks unless I can bring him to see the world *as it is today*. It is upon that we must build and not upon the stuff that beautiful dreams are made of. Wilson is blind to the actual situation, and our negotiations will fail unless he can be brought to realize that we Europeans are a tough bunch and that our problems will have to be handled with gauntlets of iron. Soft kid gloves will get us nowhere.[6]

Unable to decide between exercise of power or reliance on moral persuasion, Woodrow Wilson was, more often than not, his own worst enemy. He proved unable to help the Russians help themselves in large part because he was equally unable to help himself.

NOTES

ONE: America and Russia

1. Press release, 30 November 1918, File 882, Records of the Bureau of Foreign and Domestic Commerce, Record Group 151, National Archives (hereafter cited as BFDC, RG 151).

2. Newspaper citation from Peter Filene, *Americans and the Soviet Experiment 1917–1933* (Cambridge, Mass., 1967), p. 10; House diary, 17 March 1917, Edward House Papers, Edward House Collection, Yale University (hereafter cited as House papers or diary); House to Wilson, 17 August 1917, House papers. See also Christopher Lasch, *The American Liberals and the Russian Revolution* (New York, 1962), p. 219 (hereafter cited as Lasch).

3. Wilson speech, 11 September 1919, cited in Albert Shaw, ed., *The Messages and Papers of Woodrow Wilson* (New York, 1924), II, 871-72 (hereafter cited as Shaw); Filene, pp. 9-37; Wilson's Address to the Congress, 8 January 1918, cited in [Woodrow Wilson], *War Addresses of Woodrow Wilson* (New York, 1918), pp. 92-101 (hereafter cited as *War Addresses*); Arthur Link, *Wilson the Diplomatist* (Baltimore, 1957), p. 14 (hereafter cited as Link, *Diplomatist*); Harley Notter, *The Origins of the Foreign Policy of*

Woodrow Wilson (Baltimore, 1937), p. 223 (hereafter cited as Notter); for a study dealing specifically with the 1905 revolution see Arthur Thompson and Robert Hart, *The Uncertain Crusade: America and the Russian Revolution of 1905* (Cambridge, Mass., 1970).

4. Wilson's Address to Congress, 2 April 1917, *War Addresses*, pp. 40-41.

5. Lansing, "Non-Recognition of a Russian Government," 6 January 1918, Woodrow Wilson Papers, Library of Congress (hereafter cited as Wilson papers); see also David Hunter Miller, *My Diary at the Conference of Paris, with Documents* (New York, 1924), II, 134 (hereafter cited as Miller, *Diary*); *New York Times*, 2 December 1917; see also Henry White Plenipotentiary, Extracts of conversation between Messrs. Jenkins and Doolittle on the Russian Situation, 22 February 1919, Robert Lansing Papers, Library of Congress (hereafter cited as Lansing papers).

6. Wilson to Frank Clark, 13 November 1917, Lansing's draft press statement of 10 January 1918, and Richard Crane to Wilson, 7 May 1918, Wilson papers. Reports from Vladivostok and Riga, as late as September and October 1920, predict the imminent collapse of the Soviet regime, State Department Records Relating to Internal Affairs of Russia and the Soviet Union, 1910–1929, Record Group 59, National Archives, Washington, D.C., 861.00/7435 and 861.00/7602 (hereafter cited as 861. followed by document number); Lawrence Gelfand, *The Inquiry: American Preparations for Peace, 1917–1919* (New Haven, Yale University Press, 1963), p. 214 (hereafter cited as Gelfand); Richard Ullman, *Anglo-Soviet Relations, 1917–1921*, (3 vols: Princeton, 1961, 1968, 1972,) I, 75.

7. Frederick L. Schuman, *American Policy toward Russia since 1917: A Study of Diplomatic History, International Law and Public Opinion* (New York, 1928), p. 56 (hereafter cited as Schuman); 26 November 1917 statement sent from Washington, cited in Schuman, p. 69; official notice of the "non-recognition" of the Bolshevik regime was sent to Russia on 6 December and to American representatives in Europe and Asia on 15 December 1917. United States Department of State, *Papers Relating to the Foreign Relations of the United States, 1918, Russia* (Washington, D.C., 1931–1932), I, 289, 317 (hereafter cited as *Foreign Relations, Russia, 1918*). *New York Times*, 5 January 1918, p. 2.

8. Polk to Poole (in Moscow), 26 July 1918, 861.00/2317. This message refers to troop movements in northern Russia. Wilson to Lansing, 21 October 1918, Wilson papers. *War Addresses*, p. 98.

9. Lansing, 26 October 1918, cited in John M. Thompson, *Russia, Bolshevism, and the Versailles Peace* (Princeton, 1966), p. 15 (hereafter cited as Thompson); for information on unrest in Europe and its influence on American policy see Arno Mayer, *Wilson vs. Lenin: Political Origins of the New Diplomacy 1917–1918* (Cleveland, 1964) (hereafter cited as Mayer, *New Diplomacy*) and Arno Mayer, *Politics and Diplomacy of Peacemaking* (New York, 1967) (hereafter cited as Mayer, *Politics*).

10. See Charles Tuck's report to the State Department, 861.61/1-63; report submitted by August Heid (while employed by International Harvester), 1 July 1918, Cyrus McCormick to House, House papers.

11. Lansing to Wilson, 4 December 1919, Wilson papers; Schuman, p. 120; Herbert Hoover, *The Ordeal of Woodrow Wilson* (New York, 1958), p. 119 (hereafter cited as Hoover).

12. Daniel Smith, *Aftermath of War. Bainbridge Colby and Wilsonian Diplomacy, 1920–1921* (Philadelphia, 1970), p. 64 (hereafter cited as Smith); Sidney Bell, *Righteous Conquest: Woodrow Wilson and the Evolution of the New Diplomacy* (Port Washington, N.Y., 1972), pp. 15–16 and passim (hereafter cited as Bell); N. Gordon Levin, Jr., *Woodrow Wilson and World Politics: America's Response to War and Revolution* (New York, 1968), pp. 18–19 and passim (hereafter cited as Levin).

13. Wilson's Address to the Senate, 22 January 1917, *War Addresses,* pp. 3–12; Link, *Diplomatist,* pp. 15–16.

14. N. Gordon Levin provides the clearest picture to date of Wilson's economic thinking. While this writer feels Levin has overemphasized Wilson's materialistic consideration of pure economics, the disagreement is one of degree, not concept. See especially Levin, pp. 16–18, 26–27, 148. See also Bell, pp. 15–16, 37–38 for a very cynical analysis of Wilsonian economics; Notter, p. 55.

15. Wilson to Lansing, 23 August 1918, 861.00/2660.

16. State Department records indicate that the detailed follow-ups of cable information took two or three months to reach Washington, often too late to be of much use. The frequency with which newspapers reported the overthrow of the Bolshevik regime or the assassination of either Lenin or Trotsky gives evidence of the confused state of affairs both in Russia and in reporting. For more information on the misinformation and bias in reports from the field see Sumner Shapiro "Intervention in Russia (1918–1919)", *U.S. Naval Institute Proceedings* 99 (1973):52–61.

17. Wilson to Lamont, 31 January 1918, Wilson to Dr. Charles Eliot, 21 January 1918, and Wilson to Graham Taylor, 29 April 1918, Wilson papers.

18. Long to Lansing, 1 March 1918, "Siberia 1918," Breckinridge Long Papers, Library of Congress (hereafter cited as Long papers or diary); House diary, 26 June 1918; Bliss to Newton Baker, 22 August 1918, Wilson papers; Bliss to Baker, 14 June 1918, Box 74, Baker correspondence, Tasker Bliss Papers, Library of Congress (hereafter cited as Bliss papers); Bliss to March, 24 June 1918, Box 75, March correspondence, Bliss papers.

19. House knew that neither France nor England could meet the Wilsonian and Russian terms of no indemnities and no annexation. House to Wilson, 2 December 1918, House papers; Charles Seymour, *The Intimate Papers of Colonel House* (Boston, 1928), III, 233 (hereafter cited as Seymour); House diary, 18 December 1917. Even though the Allies were unable to agree on war aims and were wary of those Wilson might propose, they did want him to make such a statement. John W. Wheeler-Bennett, *Brest-Litovsk: The Forgotten Peace* (London: Macmillan 1956, 1938), pp. 144–45 (hereafter cited as Wheeler-Bennett).

20. Address to Congress, 8 January 1918, *War Addresses,* pp. 95-96; Arthur Walworth, *Woodrow Wilson* (New York, 1958), II, 146 (hereafter cited as Walworth).

21. George Brinkley, *The Volunteer Army and Allied Intervention in South Russia 1917-21; A Study in the Politics and Diplomacy of the Russian Civil War* (Notre Dame, Ind., Notre Dame University Press, 1966), p. xi, credits the breakup of Russia and the buildup of active resistance to the Bolsheviks to the disbandment of the Constituent Assembly.

22. Ullman, I, 128, 130. The British, according to Ullman, would have preferred having the consent of the Bolsheviks, but they were willing to go ahead without it. George F. Kennan, *Decision to Intervene* (Princeton, 1958), p. 357 (hereafter cited as Kennan, *Decision*).

23. Kennan, *Decision,* p. 382; Bliss to March, 24 June 1918, Box 75, Bliss papers. It would be easy to interpret this "hatred" as a political reflection on the nature of Bolshevism, but it is much more likely that the Allies were reacting more to Bolshevik relations with Germany than to purely ideological considerations.

24. Acting Secretary of War to Wilson, 5 March 1918, Wilson papers; Miles to Lansing, 1 July 1918, Wilson papers; Baker to Bliss, 18 July 1918, Bliss papers; Baker to Wilson, 17 November 1918, Newton Baker papers, Library of Congress (hereafter cited as Baker papers); Lansing to Morris, 9 September 1918, 861.00/2719a; Kennan, *Decision,* p. 349 and passim; Ullman, II, 8.

25. Lansing to Wilson, 11 May 1918, Wilson papers; Lansing to Francis, 14 November 1918, 861.61323/15; George F. Kennan, *Russia and the West under Lenin and Stalin* (New York, 1960), pp. 91, 98-99 (hereafter cited as Kennan, *Russia and the West*); John Silverlight, *The Victors' Dilemma: Allied Intervention in the Russian Civil War 1917-1920* (New York, 1970), p. 42 and passim (hereafter cited as Silverlight).

26. Lansing to Wilson, 21 May 1918, Wilson papers; Kennan, *Decision,* p. 356; J. B. Wright to Lansing, 29 May 1918, 861.00/2079½.

27. Louis Fischer, *Russia's Road from Peace to War: Soviet Foreign Relations 1917-1941* (New York, 1969), pp. 29-30 (hereafter cited as Fischer). Fischer cites Ullman with the suggestion that the British forced Wilson's "hand by seeing to it that the Czechs became embroiled in Siberia." This course of action had the "defect of being devious, but at least it was a means of securing the end that both they and the French desired." Fischer, pp. 25-26. See Kennan, *Decision,* for a full discussion of the events leading to Wilson's decision to intervene. On perceived need for cooperation also see House to Wilson, 24 April 1918, House papers. Also see Betty Unterberger, *America's Siberian Expedition 1918-1920: A Study of National Policy* (Westport, Conn., 1969, 1956), p. 27 (hereafter cited as Unterberger). Anyone interested in pursuing American intervention should see the 17 July 1918 *aide-mémoire* issued to the Allies and spelling out the United States' position and expectations. *Foreign Relations, Russia, 1918,* I, 287-90.

28. Bliss to Baker, 9 October 1918, Box 74, Bliss papers; Ullman, II, 86; Kennan, *Decision,* pp. 82–83; Fischer, pp. 12, 16; Ullman, II, 69; Kennan, *Decision,* p. 328; Ullman, II, 8.

29. Bliss to Baker, 25 February 1918, Box 74, Bliss papers; Long diary, 8 February 1918; House to Wilson, 10 March 1918, House papers. In July House, always working to smooth inter-Allied relations, tried to still Japanese doubts about American efforts to cut Japan out of Asia. See diary entries for 2 and 6 July 1918; J. F. Abbott to Wilson, 10 July 1918, Wilson papers; Auchincloss diary, 25 July 1918, Gordon Auchincloss Papers, House Collection, Yale University (hereafter cited as Auchincloss papers or diary).

Two: Origins of an Economic Program

1. The memorandum was enclosed in Basil Miles to Elihu Root, 8 December 1917, Elihu Root Papers, Library of Congress.

2. In his role as European relief administrator after the war, Herbert Hoover did provide food free to some regions in eastern Europe. This was not seen as part of the specifically Russian-oriented "aid" plan for Russia.

3. For brief looks at American interest in both the China and the Russian market, 1880–1920, see Marilyn B. Young, "American Expansion, 1870–1900: The Far East," and Lloyd C. Gardner, "American Foreign Policy 1900–1920: A Second Look at the Realist Critique of American Diplomacy," in Barton Bernstein, ed., *Towards a New Past: Dissenting Essays in American History* (New York: Pantheon, 1968)

4. Committee on Russian-American Relations, *The United States and the Soviet Union: A Report on the Controlling Factors in the Relations between the United States and the Soviet Union* (New York, 1933), p. 204 (hereafter cited as Committee on Russian-American Relations).

5. Creel to Wilson, 27 December 1917, George Creel Papers, Vol. I, Library of Congress. See also Lincoln Colcord to Wilson, 3 December 1917, Wilson papers; Simia Miles Romanoff to Wilson, circa February 1918, Wilson papers; Wilson to L. E. Miller, 21 March 1918, Wilson papers. S. R. Bertram to Wilson, 12 December 1917, Wilson papers; Long diary, 20 March 1918; Bertram to Lansing, 26 August 1918, Lansing papers; Merchants Association of New York to Wilson, 28 August 1918, Wilson papers; Fred Corse, of American-Russian Chamber of Commerce, 21 September 1918, 861.00/2767.

6. State Department press announcement, 26 December 1917, cited in Schuman, p. 69. (There are any number of instances in late 1917-early 1918 which suggest that neither the United States government nor its representatives inside Russia really lived up to their protestations of neutrality and noninterference. The issue is intriguing for students of Wilson's diplomacy in general but is a little outside the scope of the present study.)

7. Long diary, 29 March 1918; Long to Wilson, 4 March, and Wilson to Long, 14 March 1918, Wilson papers; Kennan, *Decision,* p. 356.

8. Long diary, 31 May 1918; Reinsch to State Department, 16 May 1918, Wilson papers; Wilson to Lansing, 20 May, and Lansing to Wilson, 21 May 1918, Wilson papers.

9. Miles memorandum, "Intervention in Russia and Siberia," 11 May 1918, 861.00/1956; see also Miles memorandum, "Non-military Measures in Russia," 3 June 1918, 861.00/2083½. As of 1914 Russia's cooperative movement had reached impressive size: 33,000 societies with a total membership of over 12 million. Credit cooperatives and agricultural producers' associations were particularly important in rural areas, significantly improving their members' chances of economic success and affluence. Richard Charques, *The Twilight of Imperial Russia* (New York: Oxford University Press, 1965), p. 198.

10. Wright to Lansing, 29 May 1918, 861.00/2079½ and Wright memorandum, 3 June 1918, 861.00/2166½.

11. Wilson to Lansing, 6 June 1918, 861.24/82; see also 861.24/84½.

12. House to Wilson, 4 June 1918, House papers; Bullitt to House, 20 May 1918, Wilson papers; see also Phillips to Lansing, 20 May 1918, 861.00/1938, in which Phillips relays a suggestion from the American League to Aid and Cooperative with Russia for the creation of a government Russian Division "to coordinate all Russian matters."

13. There is not much data on McCormick. It is very possible that he and Wilson met through Pennsylvania-New Jersey Democratic party contacts. Vance McCormick is unrelated to the other McCormick—Cyrus, of International Harvester—whose name appears in this study. Vance McCormick and House also seem to have been close acquaintances.

14. Chadbourne, Woolley, and Dulles to Chairman, War Trade Board, 5 June 1918, Box 1562, Records of War Trade Board of U.S. Russian Bureau, Incorporated, Record Group 182, National Archives (Suitland) (hereafter cited as RG 182).

15. Ibid.

16. Ibid.

17. Ibid.

18. Ibid.

19. Ibid.

20. See material filed 1 June 1918, General Correspondence, Office of the Secretary, Department of Commerce, Record Group 40, National Archives (hereafter cited as RG 40). Redfield to Wilson, 8 June 1918, Wilson papers. A 12 June Redfield to Lansing letter advising against military intervention and suggesting instead a program of economic assistance was the only formal contact between the Commerce and State departments on this matter at that time. Redfield to Lansing, 12 June 1918, 861.51/329.

21. For information on the rivalry between the State and Commerce departments, see Burton Kaufman, *Efficiency and Expansion: Foreign*

Trade Organization in the Wilson Administration 1913–1921 (Westport, Conn., 1974), pp. 77–80.

22. 13 June 1918, Wilson papers.

23. Wilson to Redfield, 13 June 1918, cited in Ray Stannard Baker, *Woodrow Wilson: Life and Letters,* 8 vols. (New York, 1939), VIII, 210–11 (hereafter cited as Baker); Redfield to Wilson, 26 June 1918, Wilson papers.

24. Wilson to Redfield, 27 June 1918, Wilson papers; Wilson to W. F. Morgan, 1 July 1918, cited in Baker, VIII, 246.

25. Miles to Phillips, 14 June 1918, 861.00/2085½.

26. Lansing to Wilson, 13 June 1918, 861.48/614 3/4a; Auchincloss's draft can be found in his papers. It should be noted that House and Auchincloss were not always able to get what they wanted from Wilson. At least partially motivated by a desire to spur some action from the president, House indulged in some machinations of his own. He wanted to satisfy the Allies' demands for intervention without running afoul of presidential or congressional opposition to a military operation in Russia. He also wanted an economic program, and he wanted Wilson to act quickly. To accomplish all of these goals, House mapped out a grandiose presidential address to Congress which would emphasize the need for increased world food production, thus laying the groundwork for a commission to Russia to assist that country in speeding up its food output. While there, the commission would take on the task of coordinating all relief activities. The commission would, of course, need "a safe and orderly field to work in," and the president should therefore tell Congress that he had "asked the cooperation and assistance" of the Allies. Congress should also be told that the Allies had given "assurance that they will not either now or in the future, interfere with Russia's political affairs, or encroach in any way upon her territorial integrity." Killing a number of birds with one stone, House thought such a program would "place the Russian and Eastern situation in [Wilson's] hands, and will satisfy the Allies and perhaps reconcile the greater part of Russia towards this kind of intervention." It would also transform the Allied push for military operations into a more economically oriented program such as many of the American policy-makers favored and about which Wilson had fewer misgivings. House to Wilson, 21 June 1918, Wilson papers.

27. Auchincloss diary, 19 and 21 June 1918.

28. Redfield to Wilson, 28 June 1918, Wilson papers.

29. Lansing to Wilson, 29 June 1918, 861.00/2219½.

30. Wilson to House, 8 July 1918, House papers.

31. Auchincloss diary, 8 July 1918.

32. *Foreign Relations, Russia, 1918,* III, 134.

33. Crane to Wilson, 23 July 1918, Wilson papers; Redfield to Wilson, 9 July 1918, Wilson papers; August 1918, General Correspondence, Office of the Secretary, RG 40.

34. House diary, 17 August 1918.

35. Lansing to Wilson, 9 July 1918, 861.00/2244A; Polk to Wilson, 5 August and handwritten note by Polk, 13 August 1918, 861.00/2569; Auchincloss to Wilson, 3 August 1918, Auchincloss papers; Auchincloss diary, 23 August 1918, Lansing to Polk, 3 August 1918, Lansing papers.

36. Wilson to Lansing, 23 August 1918, 861.00/2660; Auchincloss diary, 23 August 1918; Lansing to Jusserand, 31 August 1918, 861.00/2507.

37. House diary, 26 August 1918; Crane to Wilson, 29 August 1918, Wilson papers; State Department files, August 1918, 861.00/2741 and 2741 ½; Long memorandum, 7 September 1918 and 19 February 1919, "Siberia 1919–20," Long papers. Batolin was back in Washington in February 1919. According to Herbert Carpenter, of the American-Russian League, Batolin "is considered one of the greatest commercial and industrial leaders of the age." Carpenter to Cutler, 26 September 1918, BFDC, RG 151.

38. Cyrus McCormick to Wilson, 13 September 1918, Wilson papers. (In June the Chairman of the Red Cross mission to Romania had argued that although circumstances dictated the need for both military and economic intervention in Russia, popular sentiment in the country wanted such activities to be under American leadership in order to dispel suspicions about the other Allies. The purpose of guaranteeing American leadership would be to "preserve Russia for the Russians" and prevent incursions into Russia's sovereignty by outsiders.) See also Memorandum on Russia by Henry Anderson, no date but circa 15 June 1918, 861.00/2143.

39. British Embassy to State Department, 3 September 1918, 861.00/2619½. It should be remembered that the United States did allow England generally free play in its economic activities in northern Russia. For a brief summary of British economic activity in Siberia, see Arno W. F. Kolz, "British Economic Interests in Siberia during the Russian Civil War, 1918–1920," *Journal of Modern History* 48 (September 1976).

40. Sharp to Wilson, 8 August 1918, Wilson papers.

41. American-Russian Chamber of Commerce to Redfield, 28 September 1918, RG 40; Bullitt memorandum to Polk, 2 March 1918, Wilson papers. For more on American-Japanese relations see Unterberger.

42. Lansing to Morris, 4 September 1918, 861.00/2643a, and Lansing to Wilson, 22 August 1918, 861.00/2659; Wilson to Lansing, 26 September 1918, Long papers; State Department to Vladivostok, 26 September 1918, 861.00/2772.

43. Morris to State Department and McCormick, 2 October 1918, Box 1591, RG 182.

44. See below, pp. 64–66

45. Information on Bakhmetev's document is taken from the copy in file 245, RG 182.

46. Ibid. Ambassador Morris echoed similar sentiments when he stressed that any program would have to be experimental, taking things as they came, and directed toward practical and practicable results. Morris to State Department and McCormick, 4 October 1918, Box 1591, RG 182.

47. Association of Russian Engineers for Relief of Russia to Wilson, 30 September 1918, 861.00/2843.

48. File 245, RG 182. One wonders whether Bakhmetev had much hope that anyone—America, the Allies, or both—would or could be willing or able to undertake so sweeping a program.

49. The document most probably originated with the War Trade Board and was possibly even written by Vance McCormick. The summary presented here is from the undated, unsigned memorandum filed in Box 1552, Vol. I, RG 182.

50. Long to Lansing, 17 August 1918, 861.00/2601½; Lansing to Wilson, 29 August 1918, Long papers.

51. Lansing to Wilson, 9 September 1918, Auchincloss papers; Auchincloss diary, 9 September 1918; Wilson to Lansing, 12 September 1918, 861.48/651; Auchincloss diary, 13 and 19 September 1918. See also Wright to Miles, 22 June 1918, 861.00/2165 for evidence that the State Department saw the plight of the Czechoslovaks as a tool to force Wilson into taking some action. A committee to supervise the purchase and delivery of supplies for the Czechoslovak troops was in fact organized. A $7 million fund for that purpose was created, with the expectation that the money would be repaid by a soon to be created state of Czechoslovakia (at the time still part of the Austro-Hungarian Empire). While the Czechoslovak committee was separate and distinct from the Russian Bureau, especially in funding, there was a fair amount of cooperation between the two. For example, bureau tonnage space was allocated to supplies for the Czechoslovaks; bureau personnel worked with (and in some cases even on) the Czechoslovak committee; the bureau's Siberian field manager was asked for and did make recommendations on military as well as relief needs for the Czechoslovaks.

52. In June Wilson had told Lansing that Russian cooperative societies "may be of very great service as instruments for what we are now planning to do in Siberia." Wilson to Lansing, 19 June 1918, 861.00/2148½.

53. "Preliminary Method . . .," 23 September 1918, file 245, RG 182. In a conversation with War Trade Board—soon to become Russian Bureau—staff members, Serge Ughet of the Russian Embassy listed what he believed to be priority needs in Russia and then "laid especial stress on the necessity for distributing products in such a way as to avoid attitude of relief." He wanted the Russian people to "understand that they can procure the necessities of life if they work for them." For example, rather than sending ready-made clothing, Ughet suggested providing Russians with cloth, thread, sewing machines, etc. Memorandum on conversation with Serge Ughet, 26 September 1918, box 1582, RG 182. Ambassador Morris listed clothing, kerosene oil, sugar, hardware, agricultural implements, boots and shoes, and medical supplies as the most urgent needs. Morris to State Department and McCormick, 2 October 1918, Box 1591, RG 182.

54. House diary, 24 September 1918. In typical House fashion, the diary entry ended on the comment that Wilson "did not know that Gordon [Au-

chincloss] has worked this out and arranged it [i.e., the War Trade Board connection.]"

55. Auchincloss diary, 1, 3, and 4 October 1918.

56. Executive Order, 5 October 1918, Box 1552, Vol. I, and Corporate Records file, RG 182. There were eighteen sweepingly inclusive paragraphs enumerating possible activities, one sample of which illustrates the breadth of contingency planning: "To search for, prospect, explore, purchase, lease, or otherwise acquire, own, develop, work, operate, sell, lease, mortgage, or otherwise dispose of any and all agricultural, grazing, timber, or other lands, mineral deposits, mines, mining properties, collieries, and quarries, and the products and by-products thereof, all in any part of the world." Articles of incorporation commonly went into such detail at that time. Today they frequently simply include an omnibus clause giving the corporation authorization to do whatever is necessary in pursuit of its objectives. Certificate of Incorporation, Box 1598, RG 182.

57. War Trade Board to Heid, variously dated 3 or 10 October 1918, copies to be found in Heid cable file, RG 182, in Polk papers, and in State Department records, 861.00/29. Russian Bureau cables were usually designated as having originated with the War Trade Board (WTB), sometimes with the State Department, but never specifically from the bureau. Incoming cables were addressed to the State Department or the WTB; again, never to the bureau directly.

58. Ibid.

59. Ibid.

60. Ibid.

61. Ibid.

62. Ibid.

63. Ibid.

64. *Aide-mémoire,* 10 October 1918, Box 1550, RG 182. Sent under Frank Polk's signature, the *aide-mémoire* was drafted by Gordon Auchincloss.

65. Ibid.

THREE: Operations and Obstacles

1. Box 1598, RG 182.

2. Minutes of board meeting, 16 May 1919, RG 182; War Trade Board General Instructions 1918, Part 3, Art. III, Sec. 1, 13 December 1918, file 159, RG 151; WTB to Heid, variously dated 3 or 10 October 1918, RG 182.

3. Operating report, 1 December 1918, Box 1587, RG 182. The actual licensing applications have been destroyed, by Congressional order, and so are unavailable. There would not necessarily be any correlation between an approved license and actual shipment. There was interest among American businesses. A letter from the Bureau of Foreign and Domestic Commerce

reads in part: "Russian goods are much less "uncertain" than Russian rubles, and in fact, the market is so strong here for the raw materials that Russia can supply that firms entering into this arrangement are running not more than ordinary risks, I think. The Government's interest, of course, is in getting needed supplies into Russia; the interest of the firms sending the goods is in getting into the game early and earning good will, as much as in immediate profits." Snow to Judd, at Guaranty Trust, 16 November 1918, BFDC, RG 151.

4. Daily staff meeting, 4 and 13 December 1918, Box 1550, RG 182; Operating report, 1 December 1918, Box 1587, and Final Report, RG 182.

5. Operating report, 1 December 1918, Box 1587, RG 182.

6. Ibid.

7. Ibid.

8. Wilson to Lansing, 27 November 1918, Box 1552, Vol. I, RG 182.

9. 861.48/789; Minutes of board meeting, 14 December 1918, Box 1598, RG 182.

10. Daily staff meeting, 15 November 1918, Box 1550, RG 182. This refers to a $7 million fund established to supply the Czechoslovaks.

11. On the books, Heid was originally appointed special assistant to the Department of State attached to the American Embassy in Tokyo under the immediate direction of Ambassador Morris. He was to perform "such duties as the War Trade Board may from time to time assign" him. WTB to Heid, 10 October 1918, Box 1591, RG 182. Once in the bureau's employ, Heid managed to avoid expressing almost any political opinions. His designation as an anti-Bolshevik is based primarily on a July 1918 report written while still working for International Harvester. Report submitted by Heid to International Harvester home office in Moscow, 1 July 1918, contained in McCormick to House, House papers.

12. Morris to State Department and McCormick, 4 October 1918 and Morris to State Department and Treasury, 6 October 1918, Box 1591, RG 182.

13. Heid to WTB, 11 November 1918, RG 182.

14. Daily staff meeting, Box 1550, RG 182; File 882, BFDC, RG 151; see correspondence files with American firms, RG 182.

15. Lansing to Heid, copy to Tokyo dated 4 November 1918 (original presumably circa 28 October 1918) and Heid to State Department, 1 November 1918, Box 1591, RG 182.

16. Heid to WTB, 21 October 1918, Box 1592, RG 182.

17. Heid to WTB, 30 October 1918, Box 1592, RG 182; Polk to McCormick, 8 February 1919, Box 1552, Vol. I, RG 182. In late 1918–early 1919 Morris started "gradually depleting" the War Trade Board's forces in Japan. Morris to McCormick, 18 November 1918 and Morris to WTB, 10 January 1919, Box 1591, RG 182.

18. McCormick to Morris, 21 September 1918, cable file #11, RG 182; State Department to Heid, 5 May 1919, Box 1591, RG 182.

19. Lansing to Wilson, 17 September 1918 and Wilson to Lansing, 19 September 1918, Box 1579, RG 182; Lansing to Irkutsk, 23 October 1918,

861.00/3088a. Further impetus to such a food relief program arrived in early October from a State Department representative in northern Russia. Poole to State Department, 8 October 1918, 861.48/668.

20. Wilson to Lansing, 19 September 1918, Box 1579, RG 182.

21. Leffingwell to State Department, 19 November 1918, Box 1579, RG 182; Lansing to Wilson and Wilson to Lansing, 27 November 1918, Box 1552, Vol. I, RG 182. At the same time, Wilson also authorized transfer to the bureau of the small remaining unexpended portions of the Francis Fund. (Cole was assured that the $5 million Russian Bureau capital fund had "no connection" with the Francis or Murmansk Funds. Since he may have been party to purchases made from the Francis Fund and probably knew it was virtually depleted, and since he would be dealing with both the Murmansk and Russian Bureau funds, Cole would naturally need to be aware of the separateness of the three accounts now that they had all come under bureau authority.) Wilson to Lansing, 27 November 1918, Box 1552, Vol. I, RG 182; WTB to Cole, 24 October 1918, Box 1590, RG 182.

22. Cole to WTB, 11 December 1918, Box 1590, RG 182; Box 1551, memorandum dated 19 November 1918, "Economic Rehabilitation," RG 182: in reply to a British request that the United States ship 3,000 tons of food to Murmansk, the War Trade Board agreed but asked that the food be distributed by Cole unless the British altered their politics on the supply committee.

23. Letter, Francis to State, 27 October 1918, 861.51/436; WTB to Cole, 24 October 1918, Box 1590, RG 182.

24. Letter, C. L. Jones to Cole, 16 December 1918, Box 1594, RG 182; Cole to WTB, 8 May 1919, Box 1590, RG 182.

25. Richard Goldhurst, *The Midnight War: The American Intervention in Russia, 1918–1920* (New York: 1978), pp. 42, 188, 189.

26. Bakhmetev plan, September 1918, file 245, RG 182; Heid to WTB, 20 November 1918, 861.48/798.

27. Miles memorandum, "Intervention in Russia and Siberia," 11 May 1918, 861.00/1956 and Wright memorandum on Russia, 3 June 1918, 861.00/2166½; War Trade Board report on aid to Russia, 5 June 1918, 861.00/2085½; Bakhmetev plan, September 1918, file 245, RG 182.

28. For information on the Russian Railway Service Corps see Unterberger, passim; for correspondence relating to the origins of the commission and its first year of operations, see *Foreign Relations, Russia, 1918,* III, 183–307. For a firsthand account see John F. Stevens, "Russia During the World War," *Engineers and Engineering,* January 1927, in Roland Morris Papers, Library of Congress (Stevens's article will hereafter be cited as Stevens article; Morris papers will hereafter be cited as Morris papers).

29. Wilson to Lansing, 7 May 1917, 861.77/98½. Lansing's vision of the Corps's potential influence mirrored his broader image of a reconstructed Russia and America's role in that reconstruction. Lansing hoped that the Corps could benefit the Russian railroad workers by instilling in them a sense of "fair shop practice" and "cultivating a spirit of justice in industry." Lansing to Wilson, 5 November 1918, Wilson papers.

30. The method of financing the Russian Railway Service Corps leaves some questions as to who exactly was responsible to whom. Salaries and expenses were disbursed by the United States Treasury. Until August 1918 the Treasury made these payments from accounts allocated to the credit of the Russian Embassy—i.e., loans originally made to the Provisional Government upon which the embassy continued to draw. By August, however, those funds were running low and the ambassador asked if the United States could assume direct responsibility. Since the government wanted the Corps "to occupy the railroad management as representatives for the Russian people," direct assumption was rejected. Instead, the United States government arranged to loan the Russian Embassy the necessary funds, on the assumption that some future Russian government would reimburse these expenses. Memorandum on conversation with Russian ambassador, 30 August 1918, "Siberia 1918," Long papers; see also McAdoo to Wilson, 23 February and 16 March 1918, Wilson papers, and Miles to Polk, 17 March 1919, Polk papers.

31. Unterberger, pp. 70, 99.

32. Goldhurst, p. 42.

33. Auchincloss diary, 6 September 1918. For expressions of concern regarding Germany taking advantage of the ruble see War Trade Board report on aid to Russia, 5 June 1918, 861.00/2085½ and Treasury Department to Long, 6 September 1918, 861.00/3342. Until the armistice, most discussion involved the potential German benefits from a stable ruble; after that, concern shifted to the uses to which the Bolsheviks could put their rubles.

34. Cyrus McCormick to House, 10 June 1918, House papers; Wilson to Redfield, 13 June 1918, Wilson papers; Edward Ross, "Notes on Methods of Helping Russia," circa early 1918, Wilson papers; Redfield to Wilson, 26 June 1918, Wilson papers. See also Auchincloss diary, 19 June 1918. Miles memorandum, "Intervention in Russia and Siberia," 11 May 1918, 861.00/1956; see also Miles memorandum, "Non-military measures in Russia," 3 June 1918, 861.00/2083.

35. Currency proposal submitted by Ambassador Bakhmetev, August 1918, Wilson papers. For expressions of American support for the plan, see McAdoo to Wilson, 18 September 1918, Wilson papers, and Treasury to Long, 6 September 1918, 861.00/3342.

36. Ibid.

37. Ibid.

38. Ibid.

39. Ibid.

40. Lansing to Wilson, drafted by Long, 21 September 1918, Polk papers; File 4647/2, Wilson papers.

41. Lansing to Wilson, 21 September 1918, attached memorandum drafted by Long, Polk papers. Secretary of the Treasury McAdoo had already indicated his support of a Bakhmetev-type program to Wilson. McAdoo to Wilson, 18 September 1918, Wilson papers.

42. Rathbone to Miles, 11 September 1918, Box 1566, RG 182.
43. Auchincloss diary, 4 October 1918; War Trade Board memorandum, 5 October 1918, Box 1552, Vol. I, RG 182.
44. War Trade Board memorandum, 5 October 1918, Box 1552, Vol. I, RG 182; Francis to State Department, 27 October 1918, 861.51/436; *aide-mémoire*, 10 October 1918, signed by Polk but written by Auchincloss, Box 1550, RG 182.
45. Wilson to Lansing, 26 September 1918, "Siberia 1918," Long papers; McCormick-Polk correspondence, 22 and 25 October 1918, Box 1552, Vol. I, RG 182; WTB to Heid, 7 November 1918 relaying Board minutes for 31 October 1918, Box 1594, RG 182.
46. "Russian currency," 7 November 1918, Box 1566, RG 182. The absence of any officially recognized Russian government beyond the defunct Provisional Government made it unlikely that the Americans would accept the British format. At the same time, the United States was unwilling to sponsor any currency which could not be readily adopted by a government when such an entity did appear.
47. "Memorandum," 15 November 1918, Box 1566, RG 182.
48. "Memorandum," 15 November 1918, Box 1552, RG 182.
49. Memorandum, Thorne to Van Sinderen, 27 November 1918, Box 1566, RG 182.
50. Thorne to War Trade Board Russian Bureau, 14 December 1918, Box 1566, RG 182; Polk to London, 31 December 1918, 861.51/437.
51. Morris to State Department and Treasury, 6 October 1918, Box 1591, RG 182; Morris to State Department and War Trade Board, 4 October 1918, Box 1591, RG 182; Heid to WTB, 11 November 1918, RG 182. Always aware of the ongoing ruble depreciation, the bureau did advise Heid to exchange or expend any cash he might acquire in the course of business as fast as possible in order to avoid taking a loss. WTB to Heid, 15 October 1918, RG 182.
52. "Economic Rehabilitation," 16 December 1918 (regarding 2–12 October 1918), Box 1551, RG 182; Daily staff meeting, 19 November 1918, Box 1550, RG 182. I have been unable to determine how much business the office conducted or whether it did help put money back in circulation.
53. WTB to Heid, 12 October, 2 November and 20 November 1918, RG 182.
54. Daily staff meeting, 11 December 1918, Box 1550, RG 182.
55. WTB to Heid, 19 October and 8 November 1918, and Heid to WTB, 4 November 1918, RG 182.
56. Letter to Heid, from WTB, dated 7 November 1918, relaying minutes of 31 October board meeting, Box 1594, RG 182; WTB to Heid, 2 November 1918, RG 182.
57. WTB to Heid, 15 October and 2 November 1918, RG 182.
58. Heid to WTB, 11 November 1918, RG 182. One exception to Heid's generally negative stance on opening credits was sugar, quantities of which he does seem to have purchased through credits established with a National

City Bank branch in Vladivostok. Heid to WTB, 11 November 1918, and State Department to Heid and National City Bank, 16 November 1918, Box 1591, RG 182.

59. Heid to WTB, 11 November 1918, RG 182.

60. WTB to Heid, 15 November 1918, RG 182.

61. December Operating Report, RG 182.

FOUR: The Bureau in Limbo

1. The reader interested in secondary material on the Paris Peace Conference is directed to those works by Inga Floto, Thomas Bailey, Paul Birdsall, Stephen Bonsal, N. Gordon Levin, Arno Mayer, and John Thompson listed in the bibliography. These are not the only works available, but they serve as a starting point.

2. Lansing diaries, 26 October 1918, Harris, via Reinsch, to State Department, 16 January 1919, 861.00/3666. In November 1918 Lansing forwarded several memoranda to Wilson on the status of Bolshevism in Europe. See Wilson papers for that month; see Lansing to Root, 28 October 1918, Lansing papers, for Lansing's fear of Bolshevism; and Fosdick diary, 11 December 1918, Wilson papers, for Wilson's preconference fear of the spread of Bolshevism. Wilson quotation is from his preamble to the Prinkipo proposal, cited in Thompson, p. 4.

3. House to Lamont, 3 April 1919, Seymour, IV, 402; House diary, 8 January and 5 April 1919; see also House diary, 22 March 1919; Bliss to House, 17 February 1919, Bliss papers; Lansing to Polk, 27 January 1919, 861.00/3724; House to Wilson, 19 February 1919, House papers; report submitted to the American Peace Commissioners, 26 February 1919, Bliss papers; Bliss to Baker, 10 November 1918, Baker, VIII, 578; Bliss diary, 7 January 1919, Bliss papers.

4. Ullman, I, 153; Seymour, IV, 116; Stephen Bonsal, *Suitors and Suppliants: The Little Nations at Versailles* (New York, 1946), pp. 251–52.

5. Wilson to Grenville MacFarland, 27 November 1918, Wilson papers.

6. Lansing to Francis, 14 November 1918, 861.61323/15; Silverlight, p. 77; Bliss to Baker, 14 September 1918, Bliss papers; "Economic Rehabilitation," 16 December 1918, memorandum #3, Box 1551, RG 182; Long diary, 21 January 1919.

7. Baker to Wilson, 17 November 1918, Baker papers; see also Lansing to Francis, 14 November 1918, 861.61323/15 and Baker to Wilson, 6 November 1918, Wilson papers; Baker to Wilson, 17 November 1918, Baker papers; Baker to Wilson, 27 November 1918, Wilson papers; Graves to Adjutant General, 22 November 1918, Wilson papers.

8. Polk to Lansing, in Paris, 11 January 1919, 861.00/3628a; McCormick's recommendations contained in Baker to Wilson, 17 November 1918, Baker papers.

9. WTB to Heid, quotation taken from copy to McCormick, 26 December 1918, RG 182. See Lansing to British Chargé in Washington, 27 November 1918, 861.00/3381 and Polk to Archangel, 4 December 1918, 861.00/3220.

10. Rabbitt in Tokyo to WTB, 25 Dec 1918, Box 1591, RG 182; Polk to Lansing, 27 December 1918, 861.00/3614a.

11. Wilson to Lansing, 7 November 1918, Wilson papers; Unterberger, passim.

12. Hoover memorandum to American Peace Commissioners, 19 February 1919, House papers. See also House to Wilson, 8 November 1918, Wilson papers. For more information on the economics of America's response to Bolshevism see, for example, Levin.

13. Hoover to Wilson, 8 November 1918, Wilson papers; Bliss diary, 7 January 1919, Bliss papers; Remarks of General Bliss at the meeting of the Council of Four, 27 March 1919, House papers; see also Hoover, p. 151.

14. Outside Russia, the politics of food played an important role against Bolshevism. The Allies successfully used blockade tactics against Bela Kun's short-lived rule in Soviet Hungary. The crisis in food supplies, coupled with Romania's military attacks, forced the regime's collapse. The Baltic Provinces and Finland received extensive relief assistance, as did eastern Europe generally. Whether because of skillful use of food or for other reasons, the Allies and America did succeed in limiting Bolshevik political authority to Russian territory. On Bela Kun see George Hopkins, "The Politics of Food: United States and Soviet Hungary, March–August 1919," *Mid-America* 55 (October 1973). For more information on Hoover and food relief, see for example House diary, 11 June 1919, and Levin, p. 194. Hoover's own account, in *The Ordeal of Woodrow Wilson,* is perhaps a mite subjective. It should be noted that in this context "Russian territory" does not include Finland, the Baltic Provinces, or Poland.

15. Bakhmetev to Lansing, 14 November 1918, 861.00/3236.

16. Unsigned memorandum, 18 April 1919, House-Hoover correspondence, House papers. See also Auchincloss diary, 27, 28, 29 March, 3 April, and 15 May 1919; Hoover to Wilson, 28 March 1919, House papers; House diary 27 and 29 March, 6 and 14 April 1919; Miller, *Diary,* March through May; Hoover, passim; Poole to State Department, 21 April 1919, 861.48/835; Auchincloss diary, 15 May 1919.

17. Hoover, p. 151.

18. Daily staff meeting, 8 November 1918, Box 1550, RG 182. Van Sinderin's comment raises the question of whether (a) he was consciously trying to misdirect a public unsympathetic to government involvement in general and in Russia specifically, or (b) he truly did not see the Russian Bureau as a "special" operation.

19. Memorandum, 18 December 1918, Box 1552, Vol. I, RG 182.

20. Daily staff meeting, 11 December 1918, Box 1550 and WTB to Heid, 30 December 1918 and 3 and 20 January 1919, RG 182.

21. Memorandum by Van Sinderin and MGVD, 14 December 1918, Box 1552, Vol. I, RG 182.

22. WTB to Heid, 26 December 1918, relaying McCormick to Paris, RG 182. A 31 December cable made it clear that once a ship was out of War Trade Board control the board was no longer interested in controlling its cargo. As more and more ships fell into this category, Heid had less and less responsibility to monitor sale and distribution of goods brought into Russia, with consequently less control over the totality of American-Russian trade. WTB to Heid, 31 December 1918, Box 1591, RG 182.

23. Ibid.

24. WTB to Heid, 26 December 1918, relaying McCormick to Paris, RG 182.

25. Press release, 3 January 1919, Box 1576, and Polk to Heid, 16 January 1919, RG 182.

26. Stanert, via Polk, to McCormick, 4 February 1919, Box 1552, Vol. I, RG 182.

27. Woolley to McCormick, 28 January 1919, Box 1552, Vol. I, RG 182.

28. Reinsch to State Department, 15 November 1918, 861.00/3227.

29. J. A. Goldstein to Julius Lay, 8 November 1918, "Siberia 1918," Long papers; memorandum on conversation with Lebedev, 20 November 1918, Long papers; Long diary, 15 February 1919; memorandum regarding Batolin, 19 February 1919, "Siberia, 1919–20," Long papers.

30. A memorandum on this plan was prepared by Ellwood Kemp, Jr., and sent to Wilson on 21 November 1918, Wilson papers. For other late 1918–early 1919 suggestions for American activity in Russia see Poole to State Department, received 10 December 1918, 861.00/3374 and "Relief Plan for Russia," 14 February 1919, Box 1576, RG 182.

31. McCormick to State Department, 21 January 1919, Box 1552, Vol. I, RG 182.

32. Paris to State Department, 3 February 1919, 861.48/760.

33. General Graves also never received an updating of orders to accommodate changing conditions in Siberia.

34. See for example, Bennett, via Polk, to McCormick, 8 February 1919, Box 1552, Vol. I, RG 182.

FIVE: The Bureau in 1919

1. A. A. Boublikoff, "The Restoration of the Monetary System in Russia," published by the Russian Economic League, New York City, 1919.

2. Ibid., emphasis in original.

3. Ibid. Most of Boublikoff's readers might have found him a little melodramatic in 1919; such might not have been the case in 1931.

4. Russian Bureau, via Polk, to McCormick, 8 February 1919, Box 1552, Vol. I, RG 182.

5. In conjunction with the Red Cross, Heid responded to the "abysmal" condition of medical supplies at Omsk by requesting that the bureau "im-

mediately grant an initial credit of $1,000,000 to effect medical supplies purchases" and possibly another $1 million later for additional purchases. The loans would be made to the Red Cross, which would also distribute the supplies. Heid pointed out that the Red Cross was "the agency which has leavened if not effectively discredited anti-American propaganda" and that such a move would help "foster the good will toward Americans which the Red Cross has kept alive, as well as assist in the struggle against Bolshevism by the most certain human means." The Washington bureau office rejected bureau financing of medical supplies but did help facilitate delivery. An arrangement was worked out whereby the Russian embassy would buy surplus medical supplies from the War Department and deliver them to Russia. Heid to WTB, 4 June 1919, RG 182; Stanert to Ughet, 18 June 1919, Box 1582, RG 182; Lansing to Baker, 25 July 1919, 861.01/121a.

6. Russian Bureau, via Polk, to McCormick, 8 February 1919, Box 1552, Vol. 1, RG 182; State Department periodical reports, 24 April 1919, p. 19, Box 1553, RG 182.

7. Stanert memorandum, 1 April 1919, Box 1552, RG 182.

8. "Economic Rehabilitation of Russia," memorandum #18, Box 1551, RG 182; McCormick to WTB, 19 March 1919, BFDC, RG 151.

9. Draft, Huntington to Representative Gould, 3 February 1919, BFDC, RG 151. For evidence of some in-house bureau opposition to dealing with the cooperatives, see memorandum, 18 December 1918, Box 1552, Vol. I, RG 182.

10. WTB to Heid, 6 and 18 March and 3 April 1919, RG 182.

11. As relayed in WTB to Heid, 19 April 1919, RG 182.

12. WTB to Heid, 6 March 1919, RG 182.

13. Heid to WTB, 24 January 1919, RG 182.

14. Morris to Woolley, 17 and 28 April 1919, Box 1591, RG 182; Huntington to Gourland, 23 May 1919, File 882, BFDC, RG 151.

15. State Department periodical reports, 30 April 1919, Box 1553, RG 182; Heid to WTB, 22 April 1919, RG 182.

16. Heid to WTB, 27 March 1919 and penciled notation reading: "won't do it," RG 182.

17. Caldwell to WTB, 22 April 1919, filed in the Heid to WTB correspondence, RG 182.

18. Phillips to McCormick, 14 and 24 March 1919, Box 1552, Vol. I, RG 182. (Felix Cole, in Archangel, was apprised of the proposal to sell War Department surpluses and was asked whether there would be any interest in a similar arrangement with cooperatives in northern Russia. No further references to the idea were made, however, owing perhaps either to a lack of interest or to the imminent departure of the American troops from that area. WTB to Cole, 25 March and 15 April 1919, RG 182.)

19. McCormick to Woolley, 2 April 1919, Box 1552, Vol. I, RG 182.

20. Ibid.

21. WTB to Heid, 3 April 1919, RG 182.

22. Minutes of board meeting, 16 May 1919, RG 182.

23. WTB to Heid, 27 June 1919, RG 182. The War Department has no records of these transactions.

24. Memo #18, Box 1551, RG 182; McCormick to WTB, 19 March 1919, BFDC, RG 151.

25. Ibid.

26. Huntington to Kennedy, 3 February 1919, BFDC, RG 151; "Reconstruction—Russia," File 882, RG 151; 18 April 1919, File 411, BFDC, RG 151; Stanert memorandum, 19 March 1919, Box 1552, Vol. I, RG 182.

27. Consul in Harbin to State Department, 18 March 1919, Box 1552, Vol. I, RG 182.

28. Heid to WTB, 22 April 1919, RG 182; Caldwell to State Department, 17 March 1919, RG 182.

29. E. C. Porter to B. F. Cutler, 5 October 1918, File 882, BFDC, RG 151; Henry Green to Redfield, 5 February 1919, File 882, BFDC, RG 151.

30. This very brief summary of British activities and motivations was taken from Arno W. F. Kolz, "British Economic Interests in Siberia during the Russian Civil War, 1918–1920," *Journal of Modern History* 48 (1976): 483–91, which is itself a summary of those activities and motivations gleaned from Foreign Office records.

31. Polk to Archangel, 5 March 1919, 861.51/499; Minutes of the American Commissioners, 17 February 1919, Records of the American Commission to Negotiate Peace, Record Group 256, National Archives (hereafter cited as RG 256), 184.00101/14, RG 256; Treasury to Archangel, 25 April 1919, Box 1566, RG 182.

32. Cole to WTB, 4 April 1919, Box 1590, RG 182; Heid to WTB, 22 April 1919, RG 182. (The bureau had already suggested that, as he sold off the sample goods he had been shipped, Heid get rid of any ruble currency received in exchange as soon as possible. WTB to Heid, 6 March 1919, Box 1592, RG 182.)

33. WTB to Heid, 12 October 1918 and 18 April 1919, Box 1591, RG 182.

34. Heid to WTB, 9 and 22 April 1919, RG 182. Some of the American troops in north Russia were designated as "railroad troops" and seem to have been a kind of adjunct to the Russian Railway Service Corps. The totality of British control in that region and the impossibility of communications between Siberia and Archangel precluded much coordination. General Bliss had, in early 1919, suggested increasing the number of these troops—keeping the railroad operational was as important in the north as in Siberia—but nothing came of it. When the regular troop detachments began pulling out of north Russia, President Wilson put retention of the railroad groups on a volunteer basis. The troops did not volunteer. Bliss to Wilson, 12 February 1919, and Bliss diary, 29 July 1919, Bliss papers.

35. Unterberger, p. 109; Lansing to Paris, 22 October 1919, 861.00/5428; Schuman, p. 140. The "Russian funds at the disposal of the Russian Ambassador" were in fact American funds loaned to the ambassador specifically for the purpose of funding the Corps.

36. Stevens article.

37. Unterberger, pp. 114–15; Smith, U. S. representative to the Inter-Allied Committee, to State Department, 23 September 1919, Box 9, Roland Morris papers. (See Polk diary, 4 April 1919, for some indication of the distorted perception some Americans in Paris had of the railroad system in Russia.)

38. Cable from Morris to State Department and letter from Graves to Morris, 25 October 1918, Wilson papers; McCormick to Lansing, 8 November 1918, 861.00/3214½; Lansing to House, 2 December 1918, 861.00/6535a.

39. Draft of press release, 21 January 1919, "Siberia 1919–20," Long papers; Polk to Lansing and McCormick, 9 May 1919, 861.00/4481a; Stevens article; Unterberger, p. 117 and passim.

40. Morris to WTB, 17 and 28 April 1919, Box 1591, RG 182; letter dated 27 May 1919, File 882, BFDC, RG 151.

41. Stevens article; Unterberger, passim; Polk to Ammission, 26 April 1919, Box 1552, Vol. I, RG 182; Ammission to State Department, 5 May 1919, Box 1552, Vol. I, RG 182; Unterberger, pp. 114–17. Breckinridge Long even went so far as to suggest that the profit from the railroad could be used "in a way to re-establish credit, confidence and economic prosperity throughout Siberia." Long diary, 28 January 1919.

42. Minutes of board meeting, 16 May 1919, RG 182; Lansing to Wilson, 4 December 1919, Wilson papers.

43. Minutes of board meeting, 16 May 1919, RG 182; undated memorandum, circa June 1919, Box 1552, Vol. II, RG 182.

44. Phillips to Good, 17 June 1919, Box 1552, Vol. II, RG 182.

45. Smith to State Department, 23 September 1919, Box 9, Morris papers.

46. Commercial Attaché in Peking to Director, BFDC, 14 May 1920, File 411, BFDC, RG 151.

47. Minutes of board meeting, 16 May 1919, RG 182.

48. Ibid.

49. Minutes of board meeting, 29 May 1919, RG 182; Ammission to State Department and WTB, 28 May 1919, Box 1552, Vol. I, RG 182. (It turned out that the transfer of Francis Fund moneys, small though they were, to the Russian Bureau had, in fact, never been accomplished. The directors resolved, therefore not to accept the transfer and to request that the president rescind his order. Minutes of board meeting, 29 May 1919, RG 182.)

50. WTB to Heid, 9 June 1919, Box 1552, Vol. II, RG 182; Woolley to Treasury Department, 19 June 1919, Box 1552, Vol. II, RG 182; executive order, 24 June 1919, 861.51/620; Minutes of board meeting, 25 June 1919, RG 182; Phillips to Secretary of Commerce, 3 July 1919, File 159, RG 151. See also memorandum to Long, 8 August 1919, 861.48/932 for State Department recognition of transfer and authorization to expend funds.

51. Minutes of board meeting, 25 June 1919, RG 182; Minutes of special board meeting, 25 June 1919, RG 182. At least part of these expenses

involved stevedoring costs. See State Department to Heid, 26 March 1919 and Heid to State Department, 4 April 1919, RG 182.

52. See Statement of Assets and Liabilities appended to Minutes of special board meeting, 25 June 1919, RG 182; report on operations to June 30, 1919, and final report in liquidation, Box 1598, RG 182.

53. Report on operations to June 30, 1919, and final report in liquidation, Box 1598, RG 182.

54. Cole to WTB, 4 April 1919, Box 1590, RG 182; Minutes of board meeting, 16 May 1919, RG 182; State Department periodical reports, 24 May 1919, Box 1553, RG 182.

55. Minutes of special board meeting, 26 June 1919, RG 182; Bennett to State Department, 27 June 1919, Box 1552, Vol. II, RG 182.

56. Report on operations to June 30, 1919, and final report in liquidation, Box 1598, RG 182.

57. Cole to State Department, 11 July 1919, and Daniels to Wilson, 23 July 1919, Wilson papers.

58. State Department to Heid, 14 July 1919, Box 1591, RG 182; McCormick to Heid, 19 July 1919, Box 1591, RG 182; WTB to Heid, 27 June 1919, RG 182; Phillips to Heid, 14 July 1919, Box 1591, RG 182.

59. Phillips to Heid, 20 September 1919, 861.24/175; Heid to State Department, 20 September 1919, Long papers.

60. State Department to Heid, 7 October 1919, RG 182; Heid to WTB, 10 October 1919, RG 182. 16 December 1919, 111.70H36/3, Record Group 59, National Archives. After strenuous effort, this researcher (aided by several of the National Archives staffers) has been unable to find any records of the War Department sales to the cooperatives or of Heid's employment records with the War Department.

61. Russian Bureau to McCormick, 8 February 1919, Box 1552, Vol. I, RG 182.

62. Committee on Russian-American Relations, p. 204.

Six: Relief Proposals, 1919-1920

1. Phillips to Polk, 27 September 1919, 861.01/142; Phillips to Polk, 1 October 1919, 861.01/163a; 29 September 1919, 861.01/159; Lansing desk diaries, 20, 21, and 27 October 1919; Lansing to Omsk, 14 October 1919, 861.01/134; Polk diary, 1 October 1919; see also Lansing desk diaries, 9 October 1919.

2. The immediate cause of Wilson's displeasure with Lansing indicated a paranoia which may have been heightened by Wilson's illness and which may be discernible in his behavior during the last year of his administration. Lansing had called cabinet meetings during Wilson's indisposition and the president felt that he was engaging in something of a power play. The description of the Wilson-Colby relationship is based on Daniel Smith's

Aftermath of War: Bainbridge Colby and Wilsonian Diplomacy, 1920–1921, especially pp. 8, 11, 20, 21, and 31. Long diary, May 12, 1920. See also Wilson-Colby correspondence, Bainbridge Colby papers, Library of Congress (hereafter cited as Colby papers).

3. Smith, p. 32, see also pp. 46, 53, 54–56; Wilson to Colby, 9 and 12 November 1920, Wilson papers.

4. Schuman, pp. 156–57; Long diary, 2 August 1919; Johnson to State Department, 6 November 1920, 861.00/7642. Items 861.00/6616–6850 of the State Department records contain intelligence reports about conditions in Russia, Bolshevism, military situation, interviews with people just back from Russia, etc.

5. Smith, p. 74.

6. Phillips to Wadsworth, 4 November 1919, 861.48/977.

7. Phillips to Polk, 2 October 1919, 861.00/5308; Paris to State Department, 13 June 1919, 861.48/880; Phillips to U.S. Shipping Board, 28 October 1919, 861.48/1004; Wilson to Julius Barnes, 22 October 1919, Wilson papers. Given the date and wording, there is some doubt whether Wilson actually wrote the letter to Barnes. Its stress on propaganda is perhaps more characteristic of Joseph Tumulty than of the president. It probably did get presidential approval, whoever the actual author. See also Hoover to State Department, 7 August 1919, 861.48/918 and various documents for October in 861.48/970s and 980s. In November, DeWitt Poole reported that arrangements had been made whereby several million dollars worth of food was available in the Baltic area and General Yudenich could be sold enough of that, on credit, to feed Petrograd for a month. The American Grain Corporation was also prepared to sell 20,000 tons of grain and tonnage costs on credit if Petrograd fell. Memorandum, Poole to Assistant Secretary of State, 11 November 1919, 861.00/5879.

8. Hollyday's report is enclosed in Hapgood to State Department, 13 November 1919, 861.48/1044.

9. Harris to State Department, 19 January 1920, 861.00/6257.

10. Smith, p. 64; Ronald Radosh, "John Spargo and Wilson's Russian Policy, 1920," *Journal of American History* 52 (December 1965): 548–65 (hereafter cited as Radosh article); see Spargo correspondence in Colby papers; Spargo to Lansing, 4 November 1919, 861.00/5577.

11. Memorandum, Miles, 9 September 1919, 861.00/5461. Miles would shortly feel obliged to resign his position at the State Department, primarily as a protest against America's policy, or nonpolicy, toward Russia. Memorandum, Office of Foreign Trade Advisor to Coffin, 31 October 1919, 861.50/69 and attached note. Lansing to Wilson, 4 December 1919, Wilson papers. Much of Lansing's summary information and other material came from memoranda by DeWitt Poole, 7 and 11 November 1919, 861.00/5879 and 5884.

12. Lansing to Wilson, 4 December 1919, Wilson papers.

13. Ibid.

14. Ibid.

15. Ibid.

16. Ibid.

17. Lansing to Miss E. Herrmann, 31 December 1919, 861.48/1046.

18. Box 248, Russia, Bliss papers Baker to Bliss, 3 March 1919, 861.-602/1; Schuman, pp. 136–37; Cole to State Department, 11 July and Daniels to Wilson, 23 July 1919, Wilson papers.

19. Ullman, II, 69; House diary, 7 January 1919; for more on the unfolding of England's Russian policy in 1919 see Ullman, II, 103 and passim, and (British) "Military Appreciation of the Political Situation in West Russia," n.d. but circa late 1919, Box 78, Appendix E, Polk papers.

20. Buckler reports to House, 15 January and 10 June 1918, House papers; Baker to Bliss, 3 March 1919, 861.602/1; extract from 6 March 1919 meeting of American Peace Commissioners, Lansing papers; Wilson to Lansing, 27 May and Lansing to Wilson, 28 May 1919, Lansing papers; see also Huntington to Kennedy, 3 February 1919, BFDC, RG 151.

21. Report No. 81, "British Trade with Russia," 25 June 1919, File 448, BFDC, RG 151.

22. Lansing to London, 24 November 1919, 861.01/172; Schuman, p. 172; International Council of Premiers to Wilson, 20 January 1920, 180.03801/9; Lansing to Wilson, 20 January 1920, enclosing draft of cable from Lloyd George, Wilson papers; Davis to State Department, 7 February 1920, 861.01/189. See also Lansing to London, Warsaw, Prague, etc., 8 January 1919, 861.00/6105a; London to State Department, 28 November 1919, 861.-01/176.

23. Wilson to Polk, 4, 18, and 19 March 1920, Wilson papers; Polk diary, 8 April 1920; Polk to Eyre, 24 March 1920, Polk papers.

24. Secretary of Commerce Alexander to Polk, 24 April 1920, 861.61323/28; Geddes to Curzon, 31 May 1920, cited in Smith, p. 59; Daniels cabinet diary, 4 May 1920; see also Schuman, p. 115. Cole to Polk, 5 June 1920, 861.00/6983; Colby to London, 10 June 1920, 861.00/6983; Colby to Warsaw, 8 June 1920, 861.00/6984; Davis to State Department, 15 June 1920, 861.00/7033; State Department correspondence, July 1920, 861.-00/7121 and 7123.

25. In late August the chargé in Viborg reported that the Bolsheviks were disappointed that no contracts had yet been reached for trade with the United States. Quarton to State Department, 26 August 1920, 861.00/7279. Wilson to Davis, 23 June 1920, Wilson papers; Committee on Russian-American Relations, p. 27. For more information on the lifting of trade restrictions, see Davis to Wilson and Colby, 24 June 1920, Norman Davis Papers, Library of Congress (hereafter cited as Davis papers).

26. Davis to Colby, 7 August 1920, Davis papers; Bristol to State Department, 27 August 1920, 861.00/7252.

27. Wilson to Alexander, 11 May 1920, Wilson papers.

28. Fischer, p. 32; see also Graves, passim.

29. Daniels cabinet diary, 8 and 10 October 1919; Bristol to Polk, 15

November 1919, 861.00/5959; see also Graves and Unterberger, passim; memorandum on conversation with Russian ambassador, 4 September 1919, "Europe/Russia," Long papers; Harris to State Department, 12 April 1920, 861.00/6752.

30. Morris to State Department, 4 December 1919, 861.00/5955; see also Lansing to Wilson, 9 February 1920, Wilson papers; Thomas Lamont to Davis, 14 June 1920, Box 33, Davis papers.

31. Report from Siberia, filed in June 1920 correspondence, Wilson papers; Paris to Wilson and State Department, 29 June 1920, 861.01/223; Stevens to Colby, 11 July 1920 and Colby to Stevens, 15 July 1920, 861.00/7122. The referenced negotiations were part of an ongoing attempt to get Allied, Japanese, Chinese, and American cooperation in preserving the railroads in Russia. These negotiations and other consortium proposals —all of which carried over into the Harding administration—are discussed fully in Unterberger.

32. Smith, pp. 86–87; Smith to State Department, 24 November 1920, 861.00/7899.

33. Memorandum, Miles, 9 September 1919, 861.00/5461.

34. Memorandum, Office of Foreign Trade Advisor to Coffin, 31 October 1919, 861.50/69.

35. Note attached to 861.50/69, crediting decision to Dewitt Poole.

36. Day to Bristol, 5 November 1919, 861.00/6056; memorandum, Poole to Phillips, 7 November 1919, 861.00/5884; intelligence report sent to the State Department by U.S. Naval Forces in European waters, on Russia, 20 December 1919, 861.00/6066.

37. Mears to Kennedy, 29 October 1919, Box 2225, BFDC, RG 151.

38. Vopicka to State Department, 1 January 1920, 861.00/6073; Mac-Gowan to State Department, 9 March 1920, 861.01/203.

39. MaGruder to State Department, 13 July 1920 and Warsaw to State Department, 12 April 1920, 861.48/1170; Committee on Russian-American Relations, p. 27; MacGowan to State Department, 8 October 1920, 861.00/7501; Office of Foreign Trade Advisor, 12 October 1920, 861.00/7467.

40. See folders for October–December 1920, Box 3-B, Colby papers; Viborg to State Department, 12 January 1921, 861.00/7958.

41. Committee on Russian-American Relations, p. 204.

42. Tuck to State Department, 23 December 1920, 861.61/53.

SEVEN: Conclusion: Wilson and Russia

1. Final Operating Report, 30 June 1919, RG 182.

2. Levin, p. 191.

3. Joan Hoff Wilson, *American Business and Foreign Policy, 1920–1933* (Lexington, Ky., 1971), pp. 2–3.

4. Draft of Kennan to Lansing, 24 January 1920, Box 8, George Kennan Papers, Library of Congress.

5. Wilson, *American Business,* pp. 23 and 29.

6. Bonsal, *Suitors and Suppliants,* pp. 133–34. Italics in original.

SELECTED BIBLIOGRAPHY

The following bibliography does not pretend to be inclusive of the available literature on Woodrow Wilson's policy toward Russia. I have included those primary and secondary works which I found particularly useful in chronicling the Russian Bureau's historical context. Had the focus of the study been even slightly different, there would have been a somewhat different selection of secondary references. The source material on the Russian Bureau itself is almost entirely primary. Most of it has rested undisturbed for decades in the Suitland Annex of the National Archives. This book is the product of my belief that it is time the dust was cleared and this chapter of America's Russian policy brought to light.

Unpublished Personal Papers

Gordon Auchincloss Papers, Edward House Collection, Yale University.
Newton Baker Papers, Library of Congress.
Tasker Bliss Papers, Library of Congress.

Bainbridge Colby Papers, Library of Congress.
George Creel Papers, Library of Congress.
Norman Davis Papers, Library of Congress.
Edward House Papers, Edward House Collection, Yale University.
Robert Lansing Papers, Library of Congress.
Breckinridge Long Papers, Library of Congress.
Vance McCormick Papers, Edward House Collection, Yale University.
Roland Morris Papers, Library of Congress.
Frank Polk Papers, Edward House Collection, Yale University.
Elihu Root Papers, Library of Congress.
Woodrow Wilson Papers, Library of Congress.

UNPUBLISHED GOVERNMENT RECORDS

RG 256 Records of the American Commission to Negotiate Peace, Record Group 256, National Archives.

RG 151 Records of the Bureau of Foreign and Domestic Commerce, Record Group 151, National Archives.

RG 40 Records of the Department of Commerce, Record Group 40, National Archives.

RG 182 Records of the War Trade Board of the U.S. Russian Bureau, Incorporated, Records of the War Trade Board, Record Group 182, National Archives (Suitland Annex).

RG 59 State Department Records Relating to Internal
861.— Affairs of Russia and the Soviet Union, 1910–1929, Record Group 59, National Archives.

PUBLISHED GOVERNMENT DOCUMENTS

United States Department of State. *Papers Relating to the Foreign Relations of the United States, 1917,* and supplements. Washington, D.C.: G.P.O., 1926–32.
———. *Papers Relating to the Foreign Relations of the United States, 1918,* and supplements. Washington, D.C.: G.P.O., 1933.
———. *Papers Relating to the Foreign Relations of the United States, 1918, 1919, Russia.* Washington, D.C.: G.P.O., 1931, 1937.
———. *Papers Relating to the Foreign Relations of the United States, the Lansing Papers, 1914–1920.* Washington, D.C.: G.P.O., 1939.

PUBLISHED PRIMARY AND SECONDARY
BOOKS AND ARTICLES

American-Russian Chamber of Commerce. *Russia, the American Problem.* New York: n.p., 1920.

Bailey, Thomas. *Woodrow Wilson and the Great Betrayal.* Chicago: Quadrangle, 1945.

———. *Woodrow Wilson and the Lost Peace.* New York: Macmillan, 1944.

Baker, Ray Stannard. *Woodrow Wilson: Life and Letters.* 8 vols. New York: Doubleday, Doran, 1927.

———. *Woodrow Wilson and World Settlement.* 3 vols. Garden City, N.Y.: Doubleday, Page, 1922.

Baker, Ray Stannard, and William E. Dodd, eds. *War and Peace: Presidential Messages, Addresses and Public Papers (1917–1924) by Woodrow Wilson.* New York: Harper and Bros., 1927.

Beers, Burton F. *Vain Endeavor: Robert Lansing's Attempts to End the American-Japanese Rivalry.* Durham, N.C.: Duke University Press, 1962.

Bell, Sidney. *Righteous Conquest: Woodrow Wilson and the Evolution of the New Diplomacy.* Port Washington, N.Y.: Kennikat, 1972.

Blum, John M. *Woodrow Wilson and the Politics of Morality.* Boston: Little, Brown, 1956.

Bonsal, Stephen. *Suitors and Suppliants: The Little Nations at Versailles.* New York: Prentice-Hall, 1946.

———. *Unfinished Business.* Garden City, N.Y.: Doubleday, Doran, 1944.

Bradley, John. *Allied Intervention in Russia.* New York: Basic Books, 1968.

Carr, E. H. *The Bolshevik Revolution 1917–1923.* London: Macmillan, 1971, 1953.

Chavez, Leo E. "Herbert Hoover and Food Relief: An Application of American Ideology." Ph.D. dissertation, University of Michigan, 1976.

Committee on Russian-American Relations. *The United States and the Soviet Union: A Report on the Controlling Factors in the Relations Between the United States and the Soviet Union.* New York: American Foundation, 1933.

Cronon, E. David, ed. *The Cabinet Diaries of Josephus Daniels, 1913–1921.* Lincoln, Nebr.: University of Nebraska Press, 1963.

Davis, Donald, and Trani, Eugene. "The American YMCA and the Russian Revolution." *Slavic Review* 33 (1974), 469-91.

Diamond, William. *The Economic Thought of Woodrow Wilson.* Baltimore: Johns Hopkins Press, 1943.

Farnsworth, Beatrice. *William C. Bullitt and the Soviet Union.* Bloomington, Ind.: Indiana University Press, 1967.

Fike, Claude E. "The United States and the Russian Territorial Problems, 1917-1920." *Historian* 24 (1962), 331-46.

Filene, Peter G. *Americans and the Soviet Experiment, 1917-1933.* Cambridge, Mass.: Harvard University Press, 1967.

Fischer, Louis. *Russia's Road from Peace to War: Soviet Foreign Relations, 1917-1941.* New York: Harper and Row, 1969.

Francis, David R. *Russia from the American Embassy: April 1916-November 1918.* New York: Scribner's, 1921.

Fry, Michael G. "Britain, the Allies, and the Problem of Russia, 1918-1919." *Canadian Journal of History* 2 (1967), 62-84.

Gardner, Lloyd C. "American Foreign Policy 1900-1921: A Second Look at the Realist Critique of American Diplomacy." In Barton Bernstein, ed., *Towards a New Past: Dissenting Essays in American History.* New York: Pantheon, 1968, pp. 202-31.

―――. *Wilson and Revolutions: 1913-1921.* Philadelphia: Lippincott, 1976.

George, Alexander L., and George, Juliette L. *Woodrow Wilson and Colonel House: A Personality Study.* New York: Day, 1956.

Goldhurst, Richard. *The Midnight War: The American Intervention in Russia, 1918-1920.* New York: McGraw-Hill, 1978.

Graves, William S. *America's Siberian Adventure, 1918-1920.* New York: Cape and Smith, 1941.

Hogan, Michael J. "The United States and the Problem of International Economic Control: American Attitudes Toward European Reconstruction, 1918-1920." *Pacific Historical Review* 44 (1975), 84-103.

Hoover, Herbert. *The Ordeal of Woodrow Wilson.* New York: McGraw-Hill, 1958.

Hopkins, George W. "The Politics of Food: United States and Soviet Hungary, March-August, 1919." *Mid-America* 55 (1973), 245-70.

Kaufman, Burton I. *Efficiency and Expansion: Foreign Trade Organization in the Wilson Administration, 1913-1921.* Westport, Conn.: Greenwood, 1974.

Kennan, George F. *Russia and the West under Lenin and Stalin.* Boston: Little, Brown, 1960.

————. *Soviet-American Relations, 1917–1920.* Vol. I: *Russia Leaves the War.* Vol. II: *Decision to Intervene.* Princeton: Princeton University Press, 1956 and 1958.

Killen, Linda, "The Search for a Democratic Russia: The Wilson Administration's Russian Policy, 1917–1921." Ph.D. dissertation, University of North Carolina, 1975.

Kolz, Arno W. F. "British Economic Interests in Siberia during the Russian Civil War, 1918–1920." *Journal of Modern History* 48 (1976), 483-91.

Lansing, Robert. *The Peace Negotiations—A Personal Narrative.* Boston: Houghton-Mifflin, 1921.

————. *War Memoirs of Robert Lansing, Secretary of State.* Indianapolis: Bobbs-Merrill, 1935.

Lasch, Christopher. *The American Liberals and the Russian Revolution.* New York: Columbia University Press, 1962.

Levin, N. Gordon, Jr. *Woodrow Wilson and World Politics: America's Response to War and Revolution.* New York: Oxford University Press, 1968.

Link, Arthur. *Wilson the Diplomatist.* Baltimore: Johns Hopkins Press, 1957.

Long, John W. "American Intervention in Russia: The North Russia Expedition, 1918-1919." *Diplomatic History* 6 (1982), 45-67.

Maddox, Robert J. *The Unknown War with Russia: Wilson's Siberian Intervention.* San Rafael, Calif.: Presidio Press, 1977.

Mayer, Arno J. *Politics and Diplomacy of Peacemaking.* New York: Knopf, 1967.

————. *Wilson vs. Lenin: Political Origins of the New Diplomacy, 1917–1918.* New Haven, Conn.: Yale University Press, 1959.

Miller, David Hunter. *My Diary at the Conference of Paris, with Documents.* New York: Appeal, 1924.

Morley, James W. *The Japanese Thrust into Siberia, 1918.* New York: Columbia University Press, 1957.

Notter, Harley. *The Origins of the Foreign Policy of Woodrow Wilson.* Baltimore: Johns Hopkins Press, 1937.

Parrini, Carl P. *Heir to Empire: U.S. Economic Diplomacy, 1916–1922.* Pittsburgh: Pittsburgh University Press, 1969.

Pipes, Richard. *The Formation of the Soviet Union: Communism and Nationalism, 1917–1923.* Cambridge, Mass.: Harvard University Press, 1964.

Quirk, Robert. *An Affair of Honor—Woodrow Wilson and the Occu-*

pation of Veracruz. Lexington: University Press of Kentucky, 1962.

Radosh, Ronald. "John Spargo and Wilson's Russian Policy, 1920." *Journal of American History* 52 (1965), 548-65.

Safford, Jeffrey, J. "Edward Hurley and American Shipping Policy: An Elaboration on Wilsonian Diplomacy, 1918-1919." *Historian* 35 (1973), 568-86.

Schuman, Frederick L. *American Policy toward Russia since 1917: A Study of Diplomatic History, International Law and Public Opinion.* New York: International Publishers, 1928.

Seymour, Charles. *The Intimate Papers of Colonel House.* 4 vols. Boston: Houghton-Mifflin, 1928.

Shapiro, Sumner. "Intervention in Russia (1918-1919)." U.S. Naval Institute *Proceedings* 99 (1973), 52-61.

Shaw, Albert, ed. *The Messages and Papers of Woodrow Wilson.* New York: Doran, 1924.

Silverlight, John. *The Victors' Dilemma: Allied Intervention in the Russian Civil War, 1917-1920.* New York: Weybright and Talley, 1970.

Smith, Daniel. *Aftermath of War: Bainbridge Colby and Wilsonian Diplomacy, 1920-1921.* Philadelphia: American Philosophical Society, 1970.

Thompson, Arthur, and Hart, Robert. *The Uncertain Crusade: America and the Russian Revolution of 1905.* Cambridge, Mass.: University of Massachusetts Press, 1970.

Thompson, John M. *Russia, Bolshevism, and the Versailles Peace.* Princeton: Princeton University Press, 1967.

Trani, Eugene P. "Woodrow Wilson and the Decision to Intervene in Russia: A Reconsideration." *Journal of Modern History* 48 (1976), 440-61.

Ulam, Adam B. *Expansion and Co-existence: The History of Soviet Foreign Policy, 1917-1967.* New York: Holt, Rinehart, and Winston, 1967.

Ullman, Richard H. *Anglo-Soviet Relations, 1917-1921.* 3 vols. Princeton: Princeton University Press, 1961, 1968, and 1972.

Unterberger, Betty. *America's Siberian Expedition 1918-1920: A Study of National Policy.* Westport, Conn.: Greenwood, 1969, 1956.

Walworth, Arthur. *America's Moment: 1918. American Diplomacy at the End of World War I.* New York: Norton, 1977.

———. *Woodrow Wilson.* 2 vols. Boston: Houghton, Mifflin, 1965, 1958.

Wells, Samuel F., Jr. "New Perspectives on Wilsonian Diplomacy: The Secular Evangelism of American Political Economy." *Perspectives in American History* 6 (1972), 389-419.

Williams, Joyce G. "The Resignation of Secretary of State Robert Lansing." *Diplomatic History* 3 (1979), 337-44.

Williams, William A. *American-Russian Relations, 1781-1947.* New York: Rinehart, 1952.

Wilson, Joan Hoff. *American Business and Foreign Policy 1920–1933.* Lexington: University Press of Kentucky, 1971.

———. *Ideology and Economics: US Relations with the Soviet Union 1918–1933.* Columbia, Mo.: University of Missouri Press, 1974.

[Wilson, Woodrow]. *War Addresses of Woodrow Wilson.* New York: Ginn, 1918.

Young, Marilyn B. "American Expansion, 1870–1900: The Far East." In Barton Bernstein, ed., *Towards a New Past: Dissenting Essays in American History.* New York: Pantheon, 1968, pp. 176-201.

INDEX